PROBLEMS OF METAPHYSICS

CHANDLER PUBLICATIONS IN PHILOSOPHY
Ian Philip McGreal, Editor

Problems
of
Metaphysics

Frederick Sontag

Pomona College

CHANDLER PUBLISHING COMPANY
An Intext Publisher · Scranton, Pennsylvania 18515

For Coleman

whose name represents all past, present, and future students— without whom I could not be

CONTENTS

CONTENTS

PREFACE

Ours is a day in which every basic principle, value, and institution is under radical challenge, and thus ours is a "metaphysical age." We ought to hope that it is also a good time in which to study and to teach metaphysics, since perhaps only through such a fundamental inquiry are we likely to find once again our mental and moral orientation. In calmer days we might dispense with metaphysics without great loss, but today if we ignore it we risk total alienation from our past and from ourselves.

Nevertheless, we cannot simply start "doing metaphysics." We first have to learn how to engage in this basic inquiry. We are forced to consider our past in order to learn how to make metaphysical questions once again illuminating in the present. Since metaphysics is subject to both controversy and a variety of approaches, we cannot even examine traditional metaphysical views until we have understood how metaphysics has been dealt with in the past and that with which metaphysics now deals.

To attempt to explain metaphysics to someone else is inevitably to do it for oneself, and so my only hope is that the student will learn as much from the reading of this book as I have learned in the writing of it. For ten days, while working on the first draft of this book, I shared close quarters with several other voyagers on a ship crossing the Atlantic. We crossed the sea together and returned home as one. To learn to live together in close quarters without escape is still the major problem for us all, but the sharing of life in common makes life worth living.

F. S.

Pomona College

PROBLEMS OF METAPHYSICS

I

⚜

METAPHYSICS AS
BASIC PHILOSOPHY

Philosophy is that enterprise in which the questions we ask are always themselves fundamentally in question. That is, whenever we ask a question—for example, "Can we trust knowledge derived from the senses?"—we have to keep alert in two directions at once. We must try to answer the question, but we must also criticize the formulation of the question itself in order to discover any hidden assumptions which it may contain (such as, for example, the assumption concerning what "knowledge" is). Philosophy, insofar as it is the search for *first principles* or the basic assumptions implicit in any question, is metaphysics. It teaches us a radical form of questioning.

In this sense, "metaphysics" is simply basic philosophy, the search for and the questioning of first principles. While other fields have particular objectives—ethics, for example, is the attempt to appraise critically the norms of conduct—metaphysics alone is fundamental to every other branch of philosophy. In appraising ethical norms, for instance, one must already have uncovered the first principles upon which the norms themselves are based.

There are, unfortunately, dogmatic philosophers who resist any such critical probing into the foundation of their ideas. To be "dogmatic" is to refuse to consider whether one's ideas are clear and

1

whether they involve assumptions that ought to be challenged. Every philosopher should be a metaphysician in that he should pay critical attention to his questions and to their assumed first principles, but in point of fact not all philosophers operate in this way. Metaphysics is a special "backward-looking" form of inquiry. It is an attempt to criticize every fundamental standpoint without assuming one. As such, metaphysics is important to every mode of human existence, since metaphysicians assert that most of our practical problems actually arise from hidden differences in fundamental assumptions and not from the details of life.

Metaphysics, then, deals with problems which themselves involve even more fundamental problems, and the exasperation involved in this difficult enterprise comes from an impatient desire simply to settle a question without first reformulating and criticizing the question itself. Because of the critical restlessness occasioned by the philosopher's inability ever to settle his questions once and for all, in every philosophical inquiry philosophy as a valid enterprise is itself called into question. This continual questioning is particularly true with metaphysics. In esthetics, at least the beauty of the object does not change even if the questions about the object do, but in metaphysics we have no such enduring objects as tangible points of reference. Thus we are left with fundamental questions which themselves are constantly in question. To recognize this situation is to understand philosophy, and to reconcile ourselves to it is to answer the doubt about philosophy's usefulness.

Metaphysics, then, is a good place to fight out the battle over the meaning of philosophy, since the basic problems which we encounter in all philosophy can be seen most clearly in metaphysical terms. Metaphysics, unlike ethics, is not entangled with immediate issues (such as the moral problems involved in war) which might divert us from facing directly the challenge of the meaning and the procedure in philosophy. In the chapters which follow we will attempt to understand philosophy via metaphysics in two different ways. First, in Chapter I we will explain how metaphysics has been dealt with and discuss some of the reaons why metaphysics is always so much in dispute, even among philosophers. Then, in Chapter II we will attempt to describe the nature of the questions with which metaphysics deals. The remaining chapters will discuss eight classical philosophers. Each man will be considered with reference to the problem that concerns him most and which reveals his metaphysical position—that is, the basic perspective from which he answers questions.

The metaphysical way of thinking, it is true, does not come naturally to all men, or at least it does not do so at first; rather, it is an acquired habit. The majority of practical men operate intuitively on assumptions without challenging them. Challenge to a basic assumption tends to inhibit effective action; a nation made up entirely of metaphysicians would be in a very sad state indeed. In this sense, metaphysics is a very special enterprise which is suitable only for the critical few. Such men need careful training if this crucial work is not to degenerate into bitter attacks upon and rejections of the fundamental principles of a society or a group. Yet, for our continued intellectual health, we need to stay sensitive to the basic principles which are assumed in action, and we must have some few persons—metaphysicians—who take this need as their professional duty.

Nevertheless, all except the most fortunate of men must face metaphysical problems sometime, and everyone can profit from training in the metaphysical way of thinking whenever accepted standards come under question. When some long-perpetuated activity or moral code seems to have lost contact completely with any accepted basic principle, then metaphysical inquiry and commitment are needed to give it support again. When two ideologies which are based on quite different first principles come into conflict, what we need is not continued activity but an ability to question assumptions. This phenomenon seems to describe both our own situation and our need in the late twentieth century.

We must establish new first principles without becoming paralyzed or falling into a deep cynicism over such a basic challenge to our ways. In this immediate sense, ours is a "metaphysical generation." That is, our era is one destined to question the basic assumptions it has inherited rather than to extend their practical implications. Today, questions about society are themselves in question and no principle is beyond attack. In this case metaphysics takes on a new and an almost desperate significance. We need first to reach an understanding of our problems and then to train ourselves to deal with them. This is a skill which every classical philosopher (and every founding father of a nation) seems to have mastered before us.

A. The Nine Lives of Metaphysics

Metaphysics is a unique enterprise in the sense that one cannot simply set forth its problems and then begin to deal with them. Although we will, nevertheless, try to do something like this in the second chapter, it is best, if we are not to misunderstand meta-physics, for us to approach it negatively at first. The reason for this is the consideration already emphasized—namely, that metaphysical views are themselves always in question. Thus, in order to under-stand metaphysics properly we must begin by considering the "ques-tionable character" of the claims that metaphysicians make. The danger in doing this is that we may never get beyond negative criti-cism in order to propose positive solutions to the problems of meta-physics. A critical mental attitude or block may prevent us from understanding metaphysics as we might if we were able to move directly on to the problems as originally presented. Yet, in failing to understand why metaphysics has always questioned its own claims we would be missing a very important—and perhaps central—feature of metaphysics. In order to avoid such a negative block we will phrase the question here by asking, Why, if so many critics have dismissed metaphysics, is it still so very much alive? Our answer will tell us something illuminating about metaphysics.

Usually, when metaphysics is violently rejected and flatly refuted (when, for example, it is accused of offering unverifiable proposi-tions, say, about God), what is "killed" in this attack is only one particular metaphysical view and not all possible ones. Furthermore, if one deems the rejection to have any force, one must, at least in general, accept the basic assumptions of the view upon which the rejection is based—for example, "the verifiability principle" of the logical positivists. It becomes clear that the particular view on which this criticism of metaphysics is based—that metaphysical claims are not verifiable by sense experience—is not the only philosophical po-sition which is possible, and that the critic's assumptions have diffi-culties of their own. It is, then, impossible to reject metaphysics in general, since rejection can be done only from some one well-defined philosophical position which itself is not absolute but also open to question.

Metaphysics has more than the nine lives of the proverbial cat, then, because to attack it simply sets in motion a metaphysical process. Two things happen: First, in attacking the weak points of some metaphysical position, you only set in motion the process of attempting to formulate a more adequate metaphysics; and second, the principle upon which the rejection of a metaphysical view is based will then itself come under close scrutiny and attack. It soon becomes clear that the first principles of a critical position are nei-ther absolutely necessary nor the only ones open to philosophy. Any attack on metaphysics has the metaphysical result of calling forth an examination of the first principles of that view itself. To kill one form of metaphysics is not to do away with all metaphysics in one blow. Instead the attacker is challenged to produce a different metaphysics—that is, a set of philosophical principles as an alternative to the ones under attack.

What we learn from the fact that metaphysics refuses to die, even when some of its forms are left devastated by attack, is that it is not simply one thing. This is an unfortunate fact for those who might like to abolish it, since to argue against one form of metaphysics decisively is only to find another form taking its place. If philosophers would be so uniform and cooperative as to accept the same terms and basic definitions, then it might be possible to make a metaphysical doctrine hold still long enough to destroy it once and for all. However, it is the very heart of philosophy that its first principles are always in question and that the meaning and definition of its crucial terms (such as "knowledge") are always under discussion. This fluidity means that any attack always has the effect not of stopping the metaphysical enterprise, but of launching a basic inquiry into first principles.

B. The Platonic Tradition

Although we will begin our exposition of metaphysical views by discussing Plato's treatment of the problem of *Being*, in trying to understand metaphysics through the ways in which it has been practiced it is important to say a little about the Platonic tradition first. Although Platonists are by no means the only metaphysicians, and although many metaphysical views are opposed to Plato's (for example, Aristotle's), in a real sense it is still true that Plato is the first metaphysician of the western tradition. It is almost impossible to understand metaphysics without going back to the Platonic dialogues—even if we go back to them only in order to understand what it was that Aristotle (as Plato's pupil) reacted against. Aristotle's rejection of Platonic metaphysics itself produced, as we would expect, a new metaphysical view.

If we simply accepted all that we see at face value, we would have no need to refer to any first principles. As a matter of fact, we do not accept what is before us this easily. Instead, we are in constant dispute over our experience (see the discussion of the meaning of "justice" in the opening section of Plato's *Republic*). There are as many ways of dealing with these differences over the interpretation of experience and over the definition of important terms as there are philosophers and practical men, but Plato's particular method has been crucial in the development of what we know as "metaphysics." He suggests that it is the aspect of constant change in our experience that makes experience so difficult to accept at face value and so much subject to disagreement. Plato is convinced that change is not intelligible as such; a reference to other principles is needed if we are to understand it and to settle our disagreements about it.

What these first principles are, to which we must refer in order to comprehend the constant changes within our sense world, is an open question, and it is this question which gives rise to metaphysics. There are as many answers to the question as there are metaphysical views, but all metaphysics is in some way related to Plato's original answer: namely, that an understanding of this world does not lie within this world. Instead, real understanding requires a reference to an order which is basically different in kind from that of our natural world. This order is composed of changeless and nontemporal *Forms* (or *Ideas*) which are the archetypes of every object and concept in our world of sense. Those who have followed Plato in this quest for an order which transcends our sense world are many: Plotinus, Augustine, Anselm, Spinoza, and others. Those who have rejected this tendency are equally numerous (among them Aristotle, Hume, and Kant), but few have escaped being influenced by Plato's original solution to the problem of the unintelligibility of change when considered by itself.

We have said that since metaphysics is more than any one position it cannot be destroyed by any one argument or by anything less than an infinity of arguments. Still, in order to understand what it is that some philosophers have reacted against in metaphysics, we can and do locate certain orienting points in this enterprise that enable us to begin dealing with it. One of the most important of these points is Plato's search for a world, different in kind from the one immediately before us, by reference to which our uncertain world can be understood. If any philosopher thinks that our world is self-explanatory and not subject to dispute, then he does not construct theories about it, and if all men in practice agreed with him, we would never have such an unusual occupation as philosophy. Thus, although all metaphysical philosophers have accepted Plato's basic problem as a starting point, they have differed with him about the solution that can best produce the desired understanding of change and the resolution of our disagreement over experience.

The fact that no one theory has emerged as supreme over all others makes it still possible to consider metaphysics as a basic area of philosophy. It soon becomes clear that Plato's question can be answered in a variety of ways and that more than one set of first principles can produce understanding. Consequently, our job is now more complex and difficult. We must not only consider Plato's "world of eternal and unchanging Forms" as one suggested solution to the problem of change or *becoming*, but we must also compare and criticize other philosophical first principles in relation to this view. We cannot simply argue about the detail and the internal consistency of any philosophical position which happens to be offered to us, but instead we must analyze it until its basic assumptions or procedures become clear (for example, Plato's use of the term *Form*). Then we try to appraise these assumptions and procedures in comparison with other possible philosophical principles by considering the results of trying the various alternatives.

The fact that philosophy has not agreed on one approach or one set of concepts makes metaphysicians of all who enter philosophy—even of those who "cheat" and pretend that one set of concepts and principles is the only possible one. The Platonic tradition, then, sets our task in metaphysics for us. Plato's proposal, which posits another world—the world of *Forms*—in order to explain the world we experience, opens the question as to whether there is such a realm and, if so, what it is like. How it can be known—if it can—remains a matter of open debate in which a variety of answers is always possible. Even if the theory of Forms itself is rejected, the philosopher must come to terms with Plato, since the tradition is so ancient and powerful that it cannot be neglected and it rises afresh in each age as an alternative solution. It is also possible to reject it and to produce philosophical understanding by means which are different from Plato's. To do so is to become a metaphysician oneself and thereby to set forth first principles, even though they may be different from those to which Plato was led in order to settle the uncertainty that surrounds our experience.

C. The Quest for Certainty and Immediacy

At least in a sense, it was Plato's desire for a greater degree of certainty than our uncertain world allows which led him to accept the necessity for a world of Forms (or Ideas) different in kind from the things of our empirical world. Without changeless Forms, Plato argued, knowledge would be impossible and we would be left with nothing but shifting opinions. A form of knowledge which is to endure requires for its object a world having greater stability than the one disclosed to our senses.

Nevertheless, though Plato raised the question of how knowledge can be achieved in the face of the world's constant change, philosophers other than Plato have stressed the need for certainty more than he did. To understand their goals is to learn one more orienting fact about metaphysics as an enterprise. For although Plato's world of Forms is eternal and unchanging, it is not possible for a philosopher to write down Plato's views in a form which itself will not change or be subject to misunderstanding. Thus, the form which Platonic doctrine takes is itself far from certain.

How is it possible, other thinkers have asked, to achieve a greater degree of certainty in the formulation of philosophical doctrine itself? Many philosophers have not been content with the Platonic vision of an unchanging world which could perhaps be conceived of but not securely expressed in technical doctrine as such: they have wanted a different form of expression in order to make philosophical theories as unchanging as the Forms themselves. Plato, it seems clear, was not himself interested in having philosophers achieve one doctrine which could then be guaranteed as a certainty, but he thought that it was toward this end that the philosophical mind should be oriented. However, if we want certainty as well as a sense of immediacy, then something must be added to Plato's vision of a world of unchanging Forms as the archetypes of every object and concept in our world of sense. A different objective requires a different set of first principles.

Aristotle wanted to achieve more certainty in doctrine and a more immediate and concrete reference than Plato's world of unchanging but abstract Forms allowed. But how could this wish be accomplished? Obviously the first thing to do, as Aristotle understood, is to define the objectives of metaphysics so that they can be accomplished with certainty. When we come to discuss Plato's views on *Being* and Aristotle's views on *form*, it will be easier to understand how this can be done. In general, the way to achieve certainty is by *limitation*; that is, by limiting the objectives, the scope, and the material of metaphysics. Metaphysicians can be divided into two classes: those who set no limits on their understanding (for example, Plato and Hegel), and those who accomplish their goal by restricting it from the start to an attainable aim (for example, Aristotle and Kant).

The problem of certainty is often phrased as the problem of determining whether or not metaphysics is—or can become—a science. Since the rise of modern science the term "science" has taken on a meaning different from its classical sense. But from the beginnings of philosophy the issue has persisted as to whether metaphysics can yield a certain and rigorous knowledge. Aristotle developed metaphysics—which he called "first philosophy"—as a science distinct from the special sciences (such as biology and physics) in that "first philosophy" was regarded as the science of "being *qua* being." (It was only after Porphyry, in editing the works of Aristotle, placed the essays dealing with matters not classifiable under such traditional names as "ethics" and "physics" *after the Physics* that the problems of defining being simply *as being* were drawn together under the title "Metaphysics.")

Plato thought that our sense world is not able to yield knowledge, but it was Aristotle who wanted to turn metaphysical inquiry into a science which could yield necessary and certain conclusions. Metaphysics, as a general inquiry into the first principles of any question or discipline, may or may not seek this "scientific" goal of certainty, but the issue of the certainty of first principles always remains a central question for metaphysics.

The question of *immediacy* is one which also arises in metaphysics together with the issue as to whether metaphysics can or should seek status as a "science." If one remembers Plato's postulation of another world—a world of Forms or Ideas—to which this world must be referred in order to be understood, it is easy to understand why the problem of immediacy arises along with the question of the attainability of certainty in theory. For in spite of Plato's doctrine that all the entities of our experience "participate" in the Forms of an eternal and immutable world, it is clear that his realm of Forms is not itself immediately present to be seen, grasped, or verified. Thus, neither the existence nor the usefulness of the world of Forms can be proven in any strict sense. This impossibility means that Platonic knowledge can never yield certainty and necessity. If certainty is what we seek, then we will have to consider the question of the immediacy of the objects of metaphysics, and probably restrict metaphysics to what can be found immediately before us in experience. In seeking necessity, we want it to be impossible for the theory to be other than it is.

We will learn more later (in Chapter IV) about Aristotle's rejection of the Platonic Forms and about how he proposed to achieve immediacy for metaphysics in order to guarantee its certainty and necessity. For the present, it is enough to see that some philosophers will reject metaphysics because its objects, such as the Platonic Forms, are not immediate, while others will attempt to achieve for metaphysics the certainty of a science by restricting its range to investigations which have greater immediacy (as in Kant's critique of reason). It is easy to see how vulnerable an unrestricted range is, in that metaphysics can be rejected as being too uncertain if philosophy is allowed an unlimited range for its questions. However, the more restricted aims of metaphysics, which enable it to achieve a greater degree of certainty and necessity, always run the risk that the restrictions themselves will prove unacceptable. If they prove so, this fact destroys the certainty which is achieved by their means, and it opens up once again the basic question of the nature of metaphysics itself.

D. The Skepticism Which Cannot Be Overcome

As we have just seen, there is a skepticism about metaphysics which cannot be overcome. If, like Kant, we reject the search for any principles which are beyond experience and limit ourselves to the assumptions which reason must make in using sense experience, then a form of certainty is achieved, but the restrictions themselves which produce this certainty can always in turn come under question. For the restrictions—either of the range of metaphysics (Aristotle), or of the immediacy of its objects (Kant), or even a skepticism over allowing reason to attempt the task at all (Hume)—are themselves philosophical first principles, and each is valid only for him who accepts it as his starting point in doing philosophy. Granted that every man must use some first principle in going about philosophy, a brief study of the history of philosophy indicates that no one set of first principles or procedures is ever forced upon us. This fact leaves the doctrines of metaphysics always open for inquiry and question.

It is true, of course, that most people in most enterprises, including philosophy, do not forge their own set of premises for procedure, but rather adopt them from someone else who has already established a way of doing things. Still, the innovators in any field are those who refuse to be bound by the assumptions of someone else. They insist on leaving no premise or procedure unquestioned until, perhaps by the very fact of their rebellion, they have discovered and forged new ways for themselves and for others. This ever-present possibility of the revolutionary thinker in philosophy makes metaphysics, or the consideration of basic principles, "first philosophy," and it leaves the field always subject to a fundamental uncertainty. You never know when long-accepted principles of procedure, which provide certainty to those who do not question them, will in their turn be called into question and be subject to the basic inquiry which knows no end.

In the early twentieth century Logical Positivism sought to eliminate metaphysics by arguing that metaphysical claims are not verifiable through sense experience. Sometime earlier, Hume also had sought to limit philosophy to what could be immediately traced to some sense impression, and as long as this procedure was accepted metaphysical inquiry was rendered impossible. However, Kant challenged Hume's restrictions in order to substitute his own assumptions, and recent challenges to the premises of Logical Positivism once again launched new metaphysical inquiries. For whenever premises which were temporarily accepted are questioned, the search begins all over again for first principles in philosophy which can be accepted in their place. Restrictions are successful in producing clear, certain doctrine, but only so long as no one questions the assumptions upon which they rest. Even when these assumptions are questioned, metaphysics is not eliminated but is actually born once again.

Often skepticism about a metaphysical view arises because of a desire to test the validity of a doctrine. This approach raises the question as to the manner in which any set of first principles can be tested. We cannot review here the centuries of proposals and discussions which have been offered on this score, but it is enough to note that the issue of the "testability" of metaphysics itself gives rise to a constant form of skepticism which cannot be overcome. This impossibility holds even when a detailed test for metaphysics is actually proposed, such as the test Kant offered in his *Prolegomena to Any Future Metaphysics*. For even if a doctrine meets the proposed criteria, the *tests* of the principles can themselves be questioned. The certainty which these tests provide is subject to skepticism which arises from the possibility of doubt concerning the acceptance of the proposed standards. There are ways to overcome skepticism for the time being, and once any doctrine is accepted it is possible to achieve immunity from criticism.Unfortunately, basic principles can be questioned themselves from outside the doctrine which rests upon them; and this option produces a fundamental skepticism which no metaphysics—or antimetaphysics—can ever overcome.

One further constant source of skepticism about metaphysics concerns its *usefulness*. Many find Plato's world of Forms an intriguing idea, and others are fascinated by Spinoza's Substance, which serves as his God, but we are never sure whether or in what sense such doctrines are "useful." It is clear that the authors of such doctrines usually think that they are helpful: Plato wants philosophers to provide justice in the state through their grasp of the Forms, and Spinoza thinks that a knowledge of Substance will produce an emotional tranquility that is much to be desired in a disturbed world. However, others do not always see the usefulness of such speculative schemes. As long as it is possible to raise this question of utility—even if individual answers can be given—metaphysics will remain subject both to a basic uncertainty which cannot be overcome and to a skepticism about its value that can block its pursuit.

Often the objection about the uselessness of metaphysics arises because, in an enterprise as abstract as metaphysics, it is easy to point to many apparently useless words and unintelligible passages. This is the way in which some regard Plato's discussions of the One and the Many in the *Parmenides*. And there seems to be little doubt that philosophy in general—as well as metaphysics in particular—is prone to generate much senseless discourse in the expression of its views. The issue is not whether useless words can be found in quantity among philosophical writings, but whether among all the writings there are also passages of great insight and value. The fact that certain philosophical works are guarded, preserved, and handed down to successive generations would lead us to believe that at least a few words of great value are to be found in metaphysics. Yet, as long as men are able either to doubt this value or to point to quantities of useless philosophical theorizing, it is always possible to overlook the value which is present, and such oversight subjects metaphysics to a basic skepticism which can never be completely overcome.

In considering the question of the usefulness of metaphysics we have an opportunity to understand how a metaphysical doctrine operates. We have maintained that in understanding how metaphysical doctrine has been dealt with by various people in various times, we can also learn something about what metaphysics is and about how it works. It seems clear from our discussion that no metaphysical doctrine is itself immediate, not even Hume's definition of "impressions" and "ideas." Metaphysics may offer a doctrine which can be applied immediately to experience, but the doctrine itself is not "seen" in any way, even if the "impressions" or "sense data" are. Thus, we realize why the question of the usefulness of metaphysics will always arise again and again; we see that it does so by virtue of the kind of enterprise that metaphysics—as the positing of suggested assumptions and procedures—must be.

No doctrine, as a philosopher develops it, is immediate in any sense except that the words on the printed page are in front of the reader's eyes and some of the words at least have familiar referents. However, when the philosopher gives special meanings to certain terms (as Plato and Aristotle did in defining "Form" differently, and as Spinoza did in using the term "Substance" in a special way), then, if the philosopher is successful and the reader is imaginative and sympathetic, a theoretical structure will grow in the mind of the reader by reference to which he can interpret his own immediate experience. Still, the doctrine itself is not immediate, and those who reject or alter the premises of a metaphysical construct never see its strict applicability to experience at all. A metaphysical view, at least in certain crucial cases, may be very useful, but its status as a theory leaves it open to a skepticism which cannot be overcome—except to the degree that a given individual manages to answer the metaphysical question satisfactorily for himself.

E. The Need for a New Beginning

This search for a test of metaphysical views by which one can discover their usefulness—or uselessness—is complicated by a factor which emerges as characteristic of metaphysical theories: Even views which admittedly were once powerful and influential, if only in the intellectual sphere of ideas, have a tendency to fade and to lose their power. This phenomenon would be easy to understand if the truth were simply that a view maintains its power only in a certain age or setting and then loses it when that day has passed. A simple look at the history of philosophy, however, indicates that the fate of a theoretical system is not so easily accounted for. Sometimes new views are not readily understood and thus have little influence in their own times, while other persuasive arguments are first popular and then fade, only to become the focus of attention again and again with no apparent connection to any era (as with Anselm's ontological argument for God's existence).

We realize, then, that no metaphysical theory retains its power automatically or for any predictable period of time, and yet it can retain its power latently in the sense that it may come alive and spark new views at any time (for example, both Heidegger and Barth comment on Anselm's influence on the formation of their own thought). This renewal seems to indicate both that there is a kind of constant need for a new beginning and that there is a sense in which every time and age starts anew as if no one had thought about these issues before. The continuance of any line of theory cannot be taken for granted, since no one knows when some revolution may upset it. Metaphysics plays an important role in the constant need for a new beginning in all theoretical thinking, since it is oriented toward beginnings and seeks out first principles. It tests those principles which are assumed and it suggests new ones. The variability in the vitality of any theory, and the tendency for a theory to fade and then to be renewed, make seeking a new beginning a necessity—if we are not to be left holding onto a fast-fading theory.

Yet in additon to this timeless quality, the power and the vitality in any theoretical structure do not seem to be entirely internal to the theory. A philosopher, while working over an older theory, may discover new life and possibilites in it. Conversely, any set of first principles, when taken too much for granted, seems to lose its vitality and suggestive power for innovation. Thus, in this revitalizing process the individual metaphysician plays a crucial role, since his constant exploration uncovers latent vitality and often brings a dormant theoretical structure back to life and usefulness. This tendency to "fade away," which seems to be inherent in all theoretical structures, complicates our assessment of their usefulness. It makes it doubly difficult to be confident of any certainty which they offer, since certainty too seems subject to a loss of vitality.

This discussion also points to the fact that we are constantly dependent upon all previous theory. Since no present theory can be taken for granted, every past theoretical structure is in a sense necessary to the formation of a new one, because we never know from what undiscovered or now hidden source the suggestive and now vital spark will come to produce an innovation. We can neither assume our present theoretical context to be firm nor begin without one, and this condition involves a constant exploring and testing of all past theories for their present possibility of vitality. The fact that it is impossible for any one metaphysical system always to retain its hold places us in constant need of new beginnings. The search for first principles in order not only to root out assumptions which are no longer alive, but also to discover whether apparently lifeless premises can once again yield life to the mind in its explorations—this search is the very life of metaphysics. But metaphysics is never finished, for new beginnings are always needed.

Plainly, no previous view, when resurrected, possesses theoretical life again exactly as it did in its original form. We do not seem to achieve much in our day by accepting either Plato's theory of Forms or Kant's class of the "synthetic *a priori*." When one philosopher draws insight from another, he seldom expresses that insight in exactly the same way, and the new terms which are used are not incidental, but instead are crucial to the understanding of any philosopher's first principles. Plato does not seem to quote the pre-Socratic philosophers correctly, and Aristotle's way of talking about Platonic doctrine has puzzled historians for centuries. It seems necessary for any philosopher to alter a view in his process of appropriating it, perhaps because he sees in a previous theory something not quite on the surface, some feature which may not even have been central to the original doctrine.

We are thus constantly forced back to new beginnings. Ultimately, any suggested theory must be understood internally and on its own terms, since often what it purports to have learned from some other philosophical view is very difficult to recognize in its later, novel form. Although it is sometimes possible to see how the intense study of an earlier theory might have suggested a new view or how tampering with one part of an intricate theoretical structure may have prompted changes that ultimately led to a new theory, the matter of the life and vitality in an old metaphysical set of first principles is so complicated—as is the question of how a new theory is generated—that metaphysics is never outmoded, but instead is always with us. It returns again and again in the uncertainty generated by our constant need to find a new beginning point in thought.

II

⚜

THE PROBLEMS
OF METAPHYSICS

The approach we have used is to say that, in one sense, an inquirer cannot simply begin with metaphysical "problems." Unlike some inquiries whose questions seem obvious, metaphysics cannot be begun until the approach to it has been set, and this determination is made primarily by coming to understand how metaphysics has been dealt with in the past. Then, as an approach becomes clear for each individual concerned, the problems will begin to take shape. We discover the questions *of* metaphysics by answering the question *about* metaphysics itself as an enterprise. This procedure does not mean that there has been no continuity in the questions dealt with by metaphysicians or that these problems cannot be set forth simply—there has been and they can be. But in metaphysics the important point is not only to set forth a question and the doctrine proposed by some philosopher, but to do so in such a way that the question once again becomes meaningful.

We have to admit that the questions with which metaphysics deals are not usually meaningful when taken alone. Before they can be significant, some clear prospective about metaphysics itself must be achieved, and our suggestion is that a focus can develop as a consequence of studying how it has been dealt with in the past.

Then, each problem must be presented and understood by indicating how it arises and what the implications are of solving it in one way rather than in another. Although Aristotle has given us a near classical list of important metaphysical terms in book Delta of his *Metaphysics*—which is often called "the philosophical lexicon"—still, not every metaphysician treats exactly these same concepts, although there does tend to be a certain amount of overlap in the terminology used by each man. Thus it is important in each case to understand why certain terms, perhaps ones also significant in other writing, are made central by one author or are given crucial significance (for example, "Substance" in Spinoza and "One" in Plotinus). The problems and terms that become central often constitute a key for understanding the direction of any metaphysical doctrine.

A. Being and Nonbeing

Being and *Nonbeing* perhaps occupy a special place in metaphysical concern, though not every philosopher uses these terms as such. Aristotle defined the task of metaphysics as the consideration of "being *qua* being." There are many special sciences and disciplines, each focusing on some special area (for example, anthropology investigates the varieties and ways of man), but Aristotle thought that there should be a discipline to consider the nature of things as a whole, and not just in some special aspect. Aristotle decided that such an inquiry was possible, and his conclusion still either defines the task of metaphysics or the negation of it blocks the pursuit of metaphysics. In this respect every metaphysics concerns *Being*, since every metaphysics attempts to present the most general description of the structure of things—that is, a description which characterizes and applies to all that does or will or could exist. It is quite obvious that the question about the nature of things can be answered in different ways and that, as it is answered, so goes the direction of that metaphysics.

It should also be clear that, although a description of general structure has the widest possible application, it is difficult to make any very concrete application of the description or to verify its accuracy. The more particular and specific the inquiry, the easier it is to check the theory against the immediate facts. This inability of metaphysics to be specific, together with the difficulties of generalization, has bothered the critics of metaphysics for centuries. As you decide about the possibility for and the value of any ultimately generalized structure (for example, Leibniz' "monads," of which all things are said to be made), you also decide about the status and usefulness of metaphysics. Problems of knowledge arise next—that is, questions as to how a mind can have the scope necessary to take in, by reference to one structure, the forms of all possible things. However, it is crucial to metaphysics that the question of knowledge not be decided too quickly, particularly if such a decision artificially restricts metaphysics, until the effort to characterize Being in general terms has been made. How successful the attempt has been can be estimated only *after* the trial.

The question of Being brings up the question of Nonbeing. When we discuss the basic structures which embrace all that is, it is clear that not all existents are present at any one time. (See Section B.) Artistotle deals with this problem by means of the concept of the *potential*. Those entities or states not now actual, but which will or might become so, exist now—but only in the state of *potentiality*. As such, the structures of Being apply to them too, and this conclusion leads Aristotle to consider the means by which things "come to be" and "pass away." However, there is a more radical question than this problem of transience, and it is one which Aristotle eliminates in order to accomplish his goal of making metaphysics a completed science (see Section C). Others have been less restrictive than Aristotle and have suffered the consequences of greater uncertainty, and they have asked the question of Nonbeing in a more radical form. We will take up Plato's particular answer in the next chapter, but in order to understand the various forms of the question of Being, it is necessary first to see this question in relation to the problem of Nonbeing.

This issue can be phrased as a question concerning "the possibles." Leibniz defines "the possibles" in the widest sense as those entities or states whose conception does not involve a self-contradiction. Under such a broad definition of "possibility," it is clear that our present and future worlds present to us as actual only a small portion of the absolutely infinite extent of what is possible. Now the problem becomes to understand not only what is potential within our given natural structure, but also what relation that structure has to all possible forms of Being which could be but are not. The existence of these possibles is excluded by the fact that nature is in fact actual. "Being" has a much wider scope in that it includes more of that which *is not* than of what *is*. This inclusive scope leads to the question of how one possible structure (the world) comes to be actualized to the exclusion of all others which are possible. In this case it is the problem of Nonbeing which sets the question of Being.*

All metaphysical problems can be understood only with reference to the concrete detail of some one proposal. It is also true that in order to understand the meaning of any doctrine offered, some general opening up of the problem is needed first, since no specific concrete and visual object corresponds to the question. Thus, we have suggested that at its most comprehensive *metaphysics is the attempt to grasp the structures which include all that is or is possible.* Furthermore, although it is hard enough to describe the structure which everything that exists will exemplify, metaphysics must also go on to the even harder task of accounting for all that is not, and for how what is not came to be excluded from Being while still remaining possible in itself. This task is the search for principles which are *first*; and this is Aristotle's description of metaphysics. These principles, because they are absolutely prior, are also self-explanatory; they are explained not by reference to any other principles, but only through themselves. We can attempt to increase our understanding of such a first concept or principle, but we cannot go beyond it.

Sometimes the question of Being and Nonbeing has been taken up under the question of the *One and the Many*. (See Chapter III.) Obviously the attempt to state the basic structure of all Being (as Aristotle did through the use of the terms "form" and "matter") also represents a tendency to grasp the multiplicity of things (all that is and is not) under a greater unity and thus a simplicity. This tendency raises the question of the status of *unity* itself as a principle of Being and of whether there is such a thing as absolute unity without any multiplicity whatsoever. Sometimes the definition of philosophical reason itself has been said to be the attempt to see the unity in multiplicity and the multiplicity in apparent unity. *Reason* is the ability to discern and to articulate the relationship between the two. In any case it is clear that the function of reason will be defined by the way in which Being and Nonbeing are described and related. If philosophy is "the pursuit of wisdom or the love of rea-

* For one attempt to construct a metaphysics on this basis, see my *The Existentialist Prolegomena: To A Future Metaphysics* (Chicago: University of Chicago Press, 1969).

son," then as an enterprise it also is defined at the heart of metaphysics—that is, by means of the characterization of the structures which govern Being and Nonbeing.

B. Time and Necessity

In the attempt to talk about metaphysics' most general concern—Being and Nonbeing—the question of *time* has already been raised. In order to characterize the structure of all Being, it is clear that the present must be transcended and that we must consider both past and future together with the present. Because of this necessity, those who see reason's trustworthy side as that which is time-bound (for example, Kant) have either been suspicious about the possibility of metaphysics or have denied metaphysics altogether. Thus, in order even to take up the questions of metaphysics, we must deal with the problem of time, with the relation of the past and the future to the present, and with the mind's ability to consider all three simultaneously. Those who do not take up the question of time explicitly—its nature and the relation of human reason to it—may either reject or block metaphysics without even considering it, or else they will venture into metaphysics without understanding that one comes up against the problem of time in assuming the mind's ability to transcend the present.

There are other ways in which the problem of time is raised for metaphysics. Plato notices the instable flux which characterizes the sense world, and Aristotle notices the inevitable tendency of all things to pass away. Change seems to characterize all that man surveys, and yet perhaps some structures—those which govern all Being and Nonbeing—do not change, but are themselves the stable framework within which change takes place and is made possible. Change, the constant motion visible around us, leads to the question of time; as Aristotle observed, time seems to be "the measure of motion." Thus, in order to understand the phenomenon of change, it is necessary first to understand time—what it is, and when and to what structures it does and does not apply and how. These are important matters to determine: if any important structures are not subject to time (as, for example, Plato's Forms), and whether the mind can in any way grasp such structures or understand and deal with nontemporal orders. These questions are also crucial to the way in which metaphysics is conceived and to the question as to whether it is possible at all.

The question of *necessity* in metaphysics has many forms, but at least one of them is raised by the issue over the nature of time and its applicability to all or part of Being. For if nothing is "excused" from time's grasp, all is inevitably subject to generation and corruption, to coming-to-be and passing-away. This idea concerns the necessity of time, but it provokes the more general question as to whether necessity in one form or another characterizes all Being or, if not, then what portion of Being is so characterized. This is not an idle question for philosophy in general, for there are theories which make the possibility of philosophy dependent on the discovery of some necessary structures, since these views hold that necessity is a condition for knowledge (as in Aristotle). Later on (in Section E) we will discuss the question of *freedom* in another context, but clearly this matter is the correlative question to the issue of necessity. Spinoza and others thought that all Being must be under the control of necessity if philosophical knowledge is to be possible, but Aristotle thought that only certain essential areas need to be held firm in order to provide a foundation for knowledge.

When we attempt to describe that which provides or produces necessity ("reason" for Kant, "God" for Spinoza), we begin to build up a particular metaphysical theory. Without actually doing this here, it is still easy to see that the issue of necessity is central to all metaphysics and that the decisions made regarding this issue will direct the formation of a particular doctrine. If necessity means "that which cannot be otherwise," then accounting for it, determining its extent, and naming the forces which account for it become the core issues of any metaphysics. When we want to show that metaphysical doctrines may have crucial implications in other areas (in ethics and theology, for example), the problem of necessity is a clear illustration. For both the conduct of men and the action of God will be different and differently appraised depending on the nature and the extent of necessity.

In considering necessity, we see most clearly how metaphysics involves epistemology, or theory of knowledge. When we read Aristotle, for instance, it is clear that he works out a doctrine of necessity which governs certain areas of Being. This is not so much because his account of Being and Nonbeing requires it, but because his criteria for knowledge demand at least one area of necessity as a basis for knowledge. One can decide the requirements for knowledge (as Aristotle and Kant did) and then analyze Being in these terms. One then approaches the general structure of things with an eye to the previously established needs of a theory of knowledge. To proceed in this way is to see epistemology as an issue prior to metaphysics. As far as metaphysics as an enterprise is concerned, the question of the priority of epistemology is probably the most important procedural question to work out clearly.

On the other hand, you can hold in abeyance the question of knowledge and attempt first to give a description of the structures governing Being and Nonbeing—not temporally in this case, but in order of systematic importance. Then, with these structures made clear, the kinds and types of knowledge which are possible may be worked out. This is Plato's procedure, for instance, and in that sense he is more a primary metaphysician than Aristotle, who gave the inquiry its name. In the *Republic* Plato tells us that there are as many forms of knowledge as there are kinds of Being, and this means that knowledge cannot be characterized until we know the characteristics of the mode of Being or Nonbeing that is its particular object. The determination of the priority of epistemology over metaphysics, or the subjection of metaphysics to the established requirements of knowledge, is not a minor matter but one which is all-important to philosophy. Here again metaphysics is "first philosophy," since the determination of this issue is not an epistemological question but a metaphysical one. Although one may adopt a metaphysics unknowingly in the process of accepting the priority of a certain theory of knowledge, to do so would actually be very unmetaphysical.

C. Substance and Accident

Metaphysics has been defined, among many other ways, as the search for *substance*. Hegel suggests that what we want to know is nothing less than all things; if this is so, everything becomes essential to metaphysical inquiry. In earlier times, however, metaphysics was conceived of as a lesson in discrimination. Many facts were not thought to be worth knowing, and what we sought to know was only the *substance* of things. As we will see, Spinoza redefines this term so that it ultimately involves all things. Originally, however, "substance" meant merely that which remains constant as other characteristics change, or that which has an ability to exist independently as distinguished from properties dependent on substance for their existence (for example, there is no smile without a substantial man who smiles). Since not all things are equally transitory, the development of metaphysics depends upon locating the substantial centers of existence—those matters to which relative permanence can be attributed and which thus can provide us with a point of reference for an account of change.

The attempt to uncover substance is related to the search for *essence*— that is, for those attributes and qualities which define the thing and without which it could not be at all. *Reason* as the defining characteristic of man is a case in point. Does the special operation of reason in man distinguish him from the other animals? Is reason the essence of man's nature, as Aristotle thought? Is reason the substantial center of man's existence, a point which remains fixed while others change? Not every aspect of a thing or situation is essential. Some factors or characteristics of a thing could change and still the thing would be, while the removal of others would destroy the existence of the object. Extension, for example, is essential to all physical bodies, although a certain weight is not. If I gain or lose weight I remain alive, but if I lose the attribute of being extended, I at least do not remain the same being which I now am. In a sense these distinctions may appear obvious, but their importance lies in what they represent to the mind which is intent upon understanding Being and its characteristics.

The inquiry into both what "substance" means and what qualities are essential to the existence of the thing is a road to defining the structure of Being itself, since what we seek are the essential features of Being—that which gives Being substance. In a more general sense, such an inquiry will train the mind to dismiss unimportant features and to develop a sensitivity to those attributes which define a thing. Here we must introduce the notion of *accident*, for substance and essence cannot be distinguishing features unless there are features of any object (and also of all of Being) which are accidental—that is, features in the absence of which an object will still exist. For example, I frown instead of smile, but in doing so my existence is not threatened in the way it would be were I suddenly to lose all reason. However, not all philosophers have agreed that the world has accidental features, so that the way in which the term "accident" is treated is not incidental, but indicative of a general metaphysical position.

For one thing, the question of accidental qualities—of qualities which need not belong to an individual thing—is clearly related to the question of necessity. Aristotle thought of necessity as essential to knowledge. There must be some structures which could not be other than they are if knowledge is to have the kind of firm base he thought it required. Aristotle could accept—in fact, he proposed—a theory of accidental features that appear whenever the fortunes of chance operate. The metaphysician develops an ability to sort out the element of chance and to identify the essential features, to locate substance amidst unpredictable change. Others—Augustine, Spinoza, and Hegel—have felt that necessity must embrace all affairs and not just some, and according to such a view, strictly speaking, there are not accidents. To understand the relation between necessity and accident in a man's philosophy is to grasp one key to his metaphysics.

If the question of substance and accident revolves around the issue of whether our aim is to know all things or just an essential core, then metaphysics is a lesson in discrimination. If, however, accidents are denied and necessity takes over in every area, then our lesson in discrimination becomes that of discerning why every feature must be as it is. In such considerations the topic of the *soul* is likely to come up, and we have treated it here as a part of the question of substance and accident, whereas some philosophers place it at the heart of metaphysics, as the inquiry's most important problem. However, the central issue concerning the soul is whether it is a substance. That is, is it a focal point of existence—a center of permanence upon which other passing features of a person depend? Is the soul an essential feature of man's nature so that without it he could not be man?

One alternate response is to treat the concept of soul by reference to something else, usually by describing the behavior of the body. Plato considers the soul to be separable from the body, and as such it is a source of motion that is capable of independent existence. By way of contrast, Aristotle makes the soul the "form of a living body," and in that sense it is inseparable from the body. The point here is not the exact definition of the soul, but the status assigned to the soul in relation to the questions of substance, essence, and accident. In this sense the position taken on these three questions provides the context within which the soul can be interpreted. If this relationship is granted, then soul is not a separable metaphysical problem but is a prime example of the way in which the doctrine of essence and substance defines other crucial issues. If accidents are eliminated and necessity reigns in all areas, the soul will be denied the status of an independent source of free action. In this sense any questions concerning the soul are not answered on their own, but only after the general metaphysical structure has been determined. The doctrine of the soul as a derivative concept indicates the way in which basic metaphysical principles operate to shape the answers which become possible in other areas of philosophy.

D. First and Last Things

As we go down the list of those questions with which metaphysics deals, the issue becomes controversial as to whether the concept of metaphysics should be extended any further than we have so far indicated. That is, many would allow metaphysics to operate within the range we have already defined, but when it comes to the problems of *first and last things* (sometimes called the questions of "creation" and "eschatology"), not all metaphysicians would admit these problems to be within the scope of metaphysical concern. But Aristotle has told us that to define a thing is to set its limits, so that metaphysics becomes clear when we know where the limits to its questions are set and why all beyond that is either excluded or made the province of another discipline.

At this point the problem of the relationship of theology to metaphysics arises. For although theology may or may not concern itself with the development of technical doctrines that involve the problems outlined in the previous three sections, even if perhaps it should, still it is undeniable that theology does treat the questions posed both in this section and in the next one (on God and freedom). Of course, nothing prevents a problem from being the concern of more than one discipline. Actually this is the solution which we propose, without developing the issue of the relationship of philosophy and theology any further at this point. It is sufficient to note that at least some philosophers have treated these questions in order to support the point that a metaphysics is defined by how it approaches these questions and by where and why it sets its limits.

Plato, Plotinus, and Leibniz, for example, each gives us an account of the origin of things, although Plato labels his doctrine as a "likely tale." With this phrase he refers to the fact that, in the nature of the case, we can never check to verify any theoretical account of how the world actually came to be, since it is impossible to return to that point in time. Any account of last things will have the same status, since it is just as impossible to reach a last point as to reach a first point in order to confirm or deny a doctrine, or, what is more likely, to modify or to combine features of various theories. Nevertheless, to give such an explanation of the origin and ultimate end of the world is central to a metaphysical theory, for such an account provides the first principles that presumably shape all Being. For example, Plato's account in the *Timaeus* brings together, in a story of origin, most of the operative features of his metaphysics: soul, the Good, reason, chaos. Whatever the status of any theory as to its verifiability, it is valuable as an account of ultimate origin which sharply brings to light a philosopher's basic metaphysical principles and poses the problem of their relationship to one another.

This situation is not quite so clear where an account of last things—of the end of time—is concerned. To be sure, Plato does have such theories about the end of this world and of how it will come about, but these are mentioned less seriously than—and certainly they do not stand on a par in importance with—his account of creation. It is possible to account for the origin of things through the combination of certain basic metaphysical principles, either exemplified partially or wholly in a God or a first cause, and still leave the prediction of the ultimate end of things as an open question. Clearly this issue is of more central concern to theology, since that discipline is less free to bypass the issue. Still, either the method of treatment of eschatology or its exclusion from consideration is definitive for any metaphysics.

Interestingly enough, it is at this point that the question of ethics, or the attempt to appraise moral standards, arises in relation to metaphysics. Plato tells us that his "world maker" is ungrudging, or good, and that he therefore communicated goodness to his creation. Thus, it becomes clear that the important questions of *good* and *evil* are ultimately involved here, and in this sense no metaphysics can avoid these questions. Ethics may be an independent area of philosophy, but the basic position which metaphysics gives to the powers of good and evil certainly creates a context within which ethics takes on its significance. The issues of creation and ultimate end involve the presence of values and disvalues on a scale wider than human action and choice. We may decide to limit good and evil only to the products of human action and concern, but surely it is metaphysically important to take up the question on the wider scale of creation and eschatology first, before deciding the matter definitively.

The discussion of ultimate origin does not simply represent the idle urge of a few metaphysicians. Spinoza argues that all things are understood by tracing out their origins, and Aristotle does the same thing with his account of the causes of all things. This need to understand both origin and destiny seems to be quite basic in man, even if on technical grounds certain metaphysicians rule out the question as being beyond their scope, while those opposed to metaphysics deny the whole inquiry. At least it is clear that the restrictions are based on certain technical philosophical doctrines, whereas ordinary men take such inquiry as natural to their interests. We need to understand why our world exists in this form rather than in any one of a number of other possible forms and how the relation of good to evil is to be determined. We cannot be certain that our present order is either ultimate or everlasting. Even if we opt for skepticism regarding this matter, we need to let the questions arise and then decide either the grounds for our treatment of them or for our exclusion of them as being extraphilosophical, since on the surface they certainly appear to be at the center of philosophical concern.

E. God and Freedom

There might be some who would consider problems relating to God and freedom as being central to metaphysics. We have put these problems last in the order of things, not because we regard them as unimportant, but because these problems are prime examples of questions which cannot be treated either simply or directly; these questions need a more detailed metaphysical context before they can either arise or be dealt with at all satisfactorily. This context is necessary not because of religious restrictions, but because of the technical difficulty that God cannot be approached directly. Time and even Being are in some sense represented in our experience, but God is not. Thus, if God is to be discussed at all, this can only occur after a metaphysical context has been worked out which gives structure to such considerations. This is why antimetaphysical theologians often lose their ability to speak about God, particularly if their religious convictions grow weak. In a nonmetaphysical age, it is not possible to say much about God that will prove to have a rationally analyzable structure.

Except in a certain systematic sense that perhaps is best illustrated by Spinoza, the consideration of God is usually not first, but last in metaphysics. Aristotle's "unmoved mover" can be discussed rationally only after the context of his metaphysical scheme has been worked out (for example, his views of change). An unmoved mover may or may not be required by the metaphysical framework as a first principle, whether singly or as one among others, but this question cannot even be discussed until after the general features of the metaphysical context are known. In a sense, the questions of God's nature and his existence serve together as a catalyst which draws the various metaphysical principles into a center. What otherwise might remain as independent theories are brought into relationship when God is at issue. How the problem of God is treated is perhaps the best available indicator of the kind of metaphysics which has been developed, or at least it is a test case of the reasons behind any denial of metaphysics.

If God is not the concern of every man, and it seems clear that he is not, still the question of *freedom* is certainly one that is both vital to each human being and important in his daily conduct. Yet how can it be that the problem of freedom is also a metaphysical question which we come to only later, and never at the onset of inquiry? The answer is that in order to deal with the problem of freedom, a metaphysical context is necessary. In fact, as an intellectual question, the issue of freedom would not come up except insofar as the discussion of other metaphysical concepts (for example, necessity) seems to raise it. We also need a philosophical psychology—a theory of the soul—in order to focus on the problem of freedom in more than a vague way. Furthermore, the question of God's omnipotence has led to the question of human freedom and provided the context within which it is answered. Certainly this relationship is true for Augustine.

These considerations all amount to the fact that freedom is not a simple issue, but is the result of a number of previous metaphysical doctrines. This conclusion does not mean that we are not "free" to change our notion of freedom, but it does mean that to do so is not simply an internal matter of ethics, but actually the most arduous task in philosophy. That is, settling the question of freedom involves nothing less than the basic restructuring of the fundamental principles of metaphysics, their definition as concepts, and their relationship to one another. How the question of human freedom is decided is determined by a long chain of metaphysical decisions, so that the question of the freedom of human action depends on the freedom to shape and reshape the basic metaphysical context within which our philosophy is worked out. If we are not free to develop our own metaphysics, the problem of man's freedom will also be fixed for us. But the question of our freedom to shape a new metaphysical view for new philosophical purposes is itself the first and the chief issue of all metaphysics, and thus the issue of freedom in ethics depends on the outcome of this prior metaphysical quest for self-definition.

III

PLATO AND BEING

In the work of any metaphysician certain concepts are emphasized and employed in such a way that they provide distinctive
references by which the metaphysical doctrines that evolve can be
understood and appraised. For example, Plato's work as a metaphysician comes into focus only when you realize the degree to
which his concepts of *Being* and *becoming* provide the foundation
and distinctive character of his entire thought. We shall now attempt
to clarify the character of the work done by a number of prominent
metaphysicians by abstracting the concepts that, in each case, provide the metaphysics in question with its definitive character. Metaphysics itself can then be understood by reference to a number of
metaphysical views, each involving one or more fundamental concepts by means of which an explanatory scheme is developed and
defended.

A. Being and Becoming

If the analysis of the basic structure of *Being* (which embraces all
that is or can exist) is the central task of metaphysics, then we are
fortunate in beginning with Plato, since it was he who first raised the
question of Being and did so in an unforgettable way. Plato accom-

plished a metaphysical revolution by contrasting *Being* and *becoming*. The latter concept applies to all the visible world insofar as the world is involved in constant change and is always in the process of becoming something other than it has been. Plato found "becoming" (the world of change before us) unsatisfactory as an object of knowledge; and, since for him every form of knowledge corresponds to a type of object, he thought genuine knowledge (that is, knowledge of a kind which cannot change) must have for its object something changeless, something different from the immediate realm of becoming. Hence, Plato was convinced that knowledge must be directed to Being. For him, Being was constituted by the world of *Forms*: the patterns of all visible things, *Ideas* both eternal and immutable in their nature.

Naturally, such a realm of Being can be apprehended only by the mind, not by any physical sense. Such apprehension involves a long process of training and an education for mental discernment which is achievable only by discipline, and, even then, only by a few. However, Plato's realm of Forms, which define his realm of Being, would not be so hard to apprehend or understand if the Forms were simply the universal qualities of visible things, properties like those named by such terms as "red," "chair," and "man." But if the Platonic Forms were simply the forms of concrete things, then, Plato tells us, it would not be necessary to postulate their existence in order for them to be objects of knowledge. Actually, the qualities which concern Plato are abstract rather than concrete—such general properties as "unity," "justice," and "goodness." These abstract qualities cannot be apprehended by sight as, in a sense, such concrete properties as "man" and "chair" can. Yet we are familiar with abstract concepts, since we are constantly referring to them. Unfortunately, however, because the realm of Forms includes abstract concepts, it is a much more complicated and problematic realm than it first appeared to be. Not only do visible objects "participate" in Forms—for example, a red chair participates in both chairness and redness—but clearly, if abstract concepts are included, Platonic Forms themselves participate in other Forms. Some Forms will even apply to all other Forms. For example, unity, without a share of which nothing could be, applies to everything and also to every *thing*.

At first it seems that for knowledge to be possible one has simply to grasp the Forms in which each visible object participates. To do so would be to understand becoming in terms of Being. However, it becomes apparent that in order to understand Being itself we must go on to understand a very complex set of relations obtaining among the Forms themselves. Knowledge is seen to be complex and to involve the understanding of the following concepts: (1) which Forms can participate in each other—as, for example, "red" and "chair" can, (2) which Forms cannot participate in each other—"small" and "large" cannot (although any given object may be small in one aspect and large in another), (3) which Forms necessarily apply to all other Forms—for example, "unity" and "number," and (4) which Form orders the world of Forms itself in various ranks—namely, the Good.

At first the distinction between Being and becoming seems to be a simple one, and the world of Platonic Forms appears to provide an easy definition of Being, whether one wishes to accept the existence of Forms or not. Now knowledge of Being is recognized as a much more complicated affair, a more abstract matter than sense knowledge, and less subject to precision. Knowledge of a set of Forms, each of which is independent of the others and corresponds to some visible object or quality, is simple enough and rather easy to handle. But when Forms may share and combine and be related to each other in various ways with no outer limits set and no single pattern—that is a situation requiring for its comprehension greater complexity and agility of mind. It may even demand a mind not governed by a fixed structure but capable of flexibility and a balance of variables. Plato's definition of Being is not always understood in this more complex and slightly fluid way, but his own vision of these complications becomes quite clear in his later dialogues.

If *Being* is the central metaphysical concept in Platonic philosophy, it is nevertheless true that this term cannot be defined without reference to other concepts. Depicting that which all existent things share in common can hardly be done by reference to a single concept, and metaphysics seems unrealistic when any one particular description of Being is taken in isolation. Although the account of Being by reference to Forms is not unfair to Plato's meaning of Being, still this analysis—like those of other philosophers—is not regarded as self-sufficient. The concept of Being is recognized as standing in a context of other concepts which, when taken together, give the structure of Being a more concrete setting. In fact, although we have begun with Being, it is probably the case that this most abstract of metaphysical concepts is defined or definable only at the end of the consideration of a series of problems which lead toward it and which ultimately require a central definition of Being as a focal point for the other concepts under consideration. We move on, then, to those questions and concepts which probably in fact first led Plato to this definition of Being.

B. Being and Nonbeing

It is one thing, and a difficult enough matter at that, to find a meaning for "Being," which Plato does by contrasting Being to becoming and by opposing reason to the senses. However, it is even more difficult, but no less necessary, to give a meaning to "Nonbeing." The problem of Nonbeing arises because every attempt to characterize Being involves reference to Nonbeing. Although it is clear that many things exist, and that, as existing, they may share certain common properties, it is also clear that much which *might* be does not in fact exist and that some kinds of entities never will exist. In defining Being, we must decide whether the defining properties also prescribe Nonbeing. If so, how can it be that what accounts for the common characteristic of all that exists (in Plato's case, participation in the Forms) at the same time characterizes Nonbeing, which is surely the opposite of existence? If Nonbeing has properties, then in some sense Nonbeing must exist. But this conclusion appears paradoxical.

Although it is difficult to explain how in some sense Nonbeing "exists," it is nevertheless necessary to try to do so if we are to understand Being, and not simply leave it enmeshed in an insoluble relationship with Nonbeing. To give an account of Being, then, a description of the exact status of all which shares in Nonbeing must be included, and this complicates the problem further.

The issue of Nonbeing is raised again for Plato, interestingly enough, by his desire to define knowledge. Originally he gave his definition by associating knowledge with a grasp of the immutable Forms and with their interrelationships. Now, however, he is perplexed by those thinkers—such as the Sophists—who purport to have knowledge even though their beliefs are false. Anyone who proposes a definition of true knowledge, as Plato does, must account for those who claim to know even when their grasp of the truth is faulty. The problem of the power of false opinion (or "false knowledge") would not be such an issue if everyone but Plato were unsuccessful in the teaching of wisdom, but the obvious success of "false prophets" makes the matter of false knowledge difficult but important to explain and to deal with.

Plato regards the Sophists, or the teachers of rhetoric and practi-

cal "wisdom," as possessed of "false knowledge," and it is no accident that in the dialogue *The Sophist* Plato comes up against the
problem of Nonbeing. For if Nonbeing were simply the opposite of
Being, the difference between true and false knowledge would be
obvious, and charlatans would be successful only with fools. Unfortunately, this is not at all the case. Both life and metaphysics are
complicated affairs, and those who sincerely desire true knowledge
are often unknowingly led astray in spite of their constant alertness
for all signs of falsity. In order for the false to be taken as the true,
Plato concludes, the two must be very close together and not at
opposite poles as is usually presumed, since we are fooled when
similarities are not great, not when discrepancies are wide. We have
already seen that, according to Plato, Nonbeing must in some sense
exist and be included in Being's structures, so that perhaps the solution to the problem of "false knowledge" lies in unraveling this
metaphysical perplexity (of how Nonbeing can be said to exist).

Plato's now famous answer to the paradox of Nonbeing is that
Nonbeing exists because in addition to the positive properties which
any entity possesses, that entity is also defined by what is is not, and
in that sense it is characterized by a multitude of negative qualities.
One cannot be a man without also being not-a-woman. To be a circle
at the same time is to be not-a-square. The result of this condition is
that any object is a certain definite number of things, but there is
also an indefinite number of things which it is not—namely, every
property and characteristic other than those which define it positively. That which we are not (not-human) is thus not far from us, but
instead is actually part of our Being. We are defined negatively as
well as positively, and that which is Nonbeing makes up a large share
of our existence. Nonbeing is not far from Being and is included in
it; that is why it is so easy to pass quickly from one thing to its
apparent opposite (from being human or good or rational to being
non-human or destructive).

This account helps to explain why knowledge is so difficult to
attain and why it is so easy to be fooled when one earnestly desires
not to be. It is not a total falsity to say that someone is inhuman.
Everyone is related to the inhuman, but the issue is whether this is
most true in his mode of Being or in the mode of Nonbeing—that is,
we ask whether a person *is* inhuman or *is* not-inhuman. Then, even if
presently this quality exists in the mode of not-being, we know that
it could easily become existent. For example, a faithful husband,
who *is* a non-adulterer may become an adulterer. Thus, it is easy to
be fooled as to the exact mode of existence of any property we

consider. Because every quality actually characterizes a person in some sense, it is easy to mistake the exact relation of any description to actual existence. Words have a way of fooling us on this matter, since whatever is asserted (except a self-contradiction) could be true, in that it could pass from Nonbeing into Being as regards that person or situation.

The issue is this: Is the precise state of existence, and its relation to the indefiniteness of Nonbeing, exactly as the statement being considered says it is? We know that the statement *could* be true due to our knowledge of the intimate relation of all Being to Nonbeing and of the easy passage which is possible between them. The issue is whether or not the statement *precisely* describes the state of existence at that time, and it is impossible to tell this simply from any given assertion. Since whatever is proposed *might* be true, it is all too easy to take it as *actually* true. Only a detailed analysis of the precise state of Being and Nonbeing can help us to discern the truth, and not many have either the patience or the training for this delicate task.

If falsity were radically the opposite of truth instead of being so near to it—that is, if Nonbeing were totally nonexistent in some strange way—then it would not be so easy to be misled in knowledge or so difficult to be absolutely precise. We are misled when differences are slight and not when they are great. The cleverest people know that a near-truth is a false man's most powerful weapon. The search for Being and knowledge is made infinitely difficult by the strange phenomenon of Nonbeing's participation in existence. The Sophist slightly distorts the true relation of Being to Nonbeing. The philosopher who would uncover the pretenders to wisdom gains his power and skill by describing Being and Nonbeing with exact precision as they actually are related at a given moment, and not simply as they might be.

C. The Good and Justice

Plato's concept of Being is intended to clarify the structure of existence, but the concept has a way of getting more complicated before it gets less so. First of all, we discovered the complex relations obtaining between Plato's Forms, and then the elusive but crucial relationship of Being to Nonbeing. But, although we realize that the Forms transcend our empirical mode of existence, a further problem of transcendence arises with regard to them. When the problem of the relation that exists between the Forms arises, we can ask: Does any one principle order the relations existing between all the Forms, or the participation of Nonbeing in Being? If so, can this ordering principle be simply one Form among others, merely a part of Being itself, or must it in some way transcend both Being and the Forms themselves? If the ordering principle must transcend both Being and the Forms, we must look beyond Being and the Forms for the ultimate object of knowledge and the source of the structure of all Being and Nonbeing.

The problem of discovering the ultimate principle of order is not a simple matter, for if an infinite regress is to be avoided, a principle must be reached which is self-explanatory and self-existent. There is the further difficulty that since the Forms were originally defined as the objects of knowledge, if we are now to transcend them in the search for their ordering principle, we may be forced to transcend discursive knowledge too. This may not be difficult for a mystic, but it is very difficult for a philosopher, who is by definition "a lover of wisdom" and, hence, of discursive knowledge.

Plato, however, resolves the problem of discovering the ordering principle by introducing his famous concept of *the Good*. Although he is less than detailed in his description of this principle, it is clear that the Good stands above the Forms as their source of order, if not also as the very source of their existence. Plato admits that the Good, just because it is such a principle, must transcend Being and knowing, and this gives it a position which is important but difficult to grasp.

To prevent this tendency toward transcendence from being carried too far, in our attempt to understand Plato's metaphysics we should balance the concept of the Good with his concept of *justice*, since it is in Plato's discussion of the latter concept that the special status of the Good is defined. Plato explains knowledge and its objects and elaborates the theory of the Forms only in order to describe the source from which the administration of justice must flow. Plato is thus involved in describing a double transcendence of this world: first, the transcendence of the sense world to the unchanging realm of the Forms, and second, the transcendence of the Good beyond knowledge and Being. However, since Plato's final concern is to provide justice to the individual and to the state, his philosopher is a very practical man—a statesman and a leader of men as well as a visionary. The analysis of the world of Being is a difficult affair for Plato since it reveals complexities and the transcendence of even the intelligible world of Forms when the Good is reached. However, since Plato's metaphysics is also linked to the improvement of this temporal order, the philosopher stands with one foot in each world. Pulled in two directions, Plato must unify the two disparate realms.

The philosopher must live on two or three levels and move in two or three directions simultaneously, just as he learns from the analysis of Being that this concept also leads in several directions. Plato's analysis of the One and the Many enters in here, but essentially what must be remembered is that Being and Nonbeing, the Good, and the Forms, when fathomed metaphysically, yield the key to understanding the practical world. It is not the other way around. A grasp of Being's structure makes possible powerful and precise practical action; at least, it does so if justice rather than blind tyranny is our aim.

The "good life" for Plato is a mixed enterprise and not a tendency toward purity alone. Thus justice requires an understanding of the principles of mixture; this fact will become important by contrast to the view held by Plotinus (see Chapter V). In the *Philebus* Plato discusses the life of pleasure, and he decides that it cannot be at its best without the inclusion of knowledge. But we already know enough about the intricacies of Plato's theory of knowledge to suspect that pleasure and the good life will turn out to be complex blends too. Still, there are good and bad mixtures, and Plato's goal turns out to be "the well-mixed life." If we know the problems involved in the combination of the Forms, then we can see that the standard for this "mixture" of pleasures will depend on a precise knowledge of the structure of Being and Nonbeing, the Forms, and the transcendent Good. Plato's good life is a compromise between a tendency to transcend the world of sense and the tendency to regard the world of sense as ultimate.

It is not easy to live in a land "in-between," although Plato recommends such a life as best. It is not easy to have knowledge both attached to and oriented back toward the sense world and still have it also tend to absolute transcendence in the Good. Nor is it easy to have Being involved in Nonbeing, or falsity so closely related to truth. These difficulties are perhaps why so many critics have tended to make the error of interpreting Plato's metaphysics as fixed in one definite position rather than as definitely committed to a mixed life. Because so many competing tendencies are present in Plato's metaphysics, although contemporary metaphysicians constantly return to Plato as a source, they often reject features of his doctrine, since Plato was himself unable to hold all of its complex and opposing parts in relationship at once.

D. The Soul and Reason

Because of the delicate balances involved in the ordering of Plato's metaphysical principles and their tendency in themselves to split apart, it is clear that neither the tension between Being and Nonbeing as the relation between the Forms, nor the Good as a transcendent principle, is really sufficient to account for the world we find before us. Another principle is needed to finish the account, and some have argued that this further principle is the key to Platonic metaphysics—more significant, perhaps, than the more celebrated doctrine of the Forms. *Soul* is the crucial factor still needed to make this metaphysics work, and Plato gives this concept a place of prominence. The characteristics of soul are different, as we might suspect, from those which define the Forms. The soul is a principle of motion and, more than that, it is a self-mover. It accounts for the motion of other things, but in itself it is an original source of motion. Since the soul is the principle of motion, it involves self-existence, and this means that the Platonic Forms share the status of being eternal with something quite different from themselves: namely, souls.

Because of the static nature of the Forms, motion does not have its source there, even though at times the participation of Forms in each other seems to be a kind of source of motion. *Soul* is that which initiates and explains motion, although it does not do this in all situations, but only in those which are orderly, purposeful, and directed. Chaos breeds a kind of blind and random motion, and in Plato's account of creation this uncontrolled motion is regarded as originating in what Plato calls "the receptacle" of all things. Of the two forms of motion, the uncontrolled and the ordered, it is ordered motion which is the more important, and this type is the product of soul. Ordered motion is not an automatic product, however, for Plato knows too well that souls can run amuck. Only the soul under rational guidance can be the source of desirable motion; even souls can be dominated by irrational forces and can produce destruction and chaos. The soul has desires and passions, and these must be held in a delicate balance by rational control if the soul is to produce motion which is desirable.

Still, even at this stage Plato's doctrine is not uncomplicated, for Plato knows that souls are sometimes affected by forces outside themselves. It would be easy to say that all such external dominance of the soul is a madness to be avoided, but again Plato does not take the easy way out. Some nonrational forces lift the soul to heights of vision without which it might remain uncreative and pedestrian, even though rational. We must distinguish divine from demoniac possession; inspiration comes when the soul is literally lifted out of itself. Even the Good transcends Being at times, and the soul is best when it is lifted out of itself—as long as it is under rational control. Occasionally the soul is inspired by a "divine madness" capable of tearing it loose from its enmeshed state. If we reject all irrationality, therefore, we might stifle the very force capable of inspiring the soul to achievements which otherwise would be impossible. Nevertheless, this consideration does not make all irrational influence good. Some possessive forces are destructive and distorting, and the governance of the soul is thus no easy matter, just as it is not easy to apprehend the Good beyond Being.

In the same way that the soul is the source of motion for Plato, it is also the source of creativity. No Form is of itself productive, except for the complicating fact that the Good tends toward self-communication. *Reason* is a principle which although not identical with the soul, is a part of its life; and it serves as the link between soul and the Forms, since reason is defined as the faculty capable of apprehending such intellectual entities and grasping relationships. By being able to comprehend these relationships, reason is able to introduce order into what it governs, to bring justice to the state, and to infuse into the soul the subtle grasp of the mixture that constitutes the good life. Soul, so different in kind from the world of Forms, is joined with them through the soul's ability to reason, which links the soul to the qualities that the Forms embody. Yet, because the soul is also closely associated with the qualities of physical and sensuous life, simple reason is not always enough to shake the soul loose or to raise it to the vision which it needs. This is the point at which the dangerous quality of "divine madness" (or inspiration of the sort that moves poets) is dangerous, because it is so much like the kinds of irrational possession which can destroy the soul. Such are, however, the risks of being a creature of mixed qualities, which man is.

E. The One and the Many

In a way, all of Plato's metaphysics can be seen as summarized in capsule form in his account of *the One and the Many* in the *Parmenides*. Not everyone will see this dialogue as occupying a central place in Plato's thought, and it is clear that one needs a familiarity with the details of Plato's writing before the significance of the problem of the One and the Many can be appreciated. Still, some take the problem of unity and multiplicity as the core of all metaphysics, and, as we will see, it is concerning the One and the Many that Plotinus differs so radically and so importantly from Plato. However, Plato gives us no explicit conclusion to the problem of the One and the Many; hence each reader must determine the answer for himself— which perhaps in itself is a decisive clue to Plato's metaphysical procedure.

What Plato suggests is that the One, if it is left unqualified, is beyond either knowing or discourse. Sheer unity is not describable, except that it must be *other than* the Many. The One, then, has a second quality after sheer unity, a quality which links its very nature to the Many; namely, the quality of being other than the Many. Yet, similarly, the Many, in order to be many, must be "one many"—that is, other than sheer unity—and each of its many components must be one thing. Through the concept of *otherness*, it seems, the One and the Many are indissolubly linked. Each exists in a fluid state and tends on the one hand toward indefinite multiplicity (chaos), and on the other hand toward a sheer unity (beyond Being and knowledge).

What can stabilize such a fluctuating situation, a shifting world which seems unable to find a point of rest by itself? Here reason and the soul, together with the complex relations which we have discerned as existing between Being and Nonbeing, all enter in. Plato began his account with a presentation of the difficulties inherent in the doctrine of the Forms, and he suggested that the solution depended upon reaching some insight into the relation between the One and the Many. Now Plato has discovered that the One and the Many are indissolubly related to each other and that unity naturally moves toward multiplicity, and vice versa. Here we meet the famous doctrine of the "golden mean," which was to be made classical in ethical theory by Aristotle. One must, through reason and the soul, neither let unity dominate nor allow multiplicity to move toward indefiniteness. Instead, the oscillation must be held at some definite number, stopped at some mean between extremes.

By its constitution, then, the world tends constantly toward either one extreme or another. If the tendency to extremes is to be controlled, it can be accomplished only by human intervention, through the rational control of the soul. The elements of the world, which in themselves are without fixed limits, have actually had limits set upon them in order to form a universe by the intervention and mediation of a world-making soul. In the same way the elements in our life tend of themselves either toward one extreme or another, unless they are constantly held in control. Order and goodness are, however, introduced only by ever alert, subtle judgment and balance, which ultimately are founded on a metaphysical apprehension of the basic elements of our world. In the Platonic scheme this ordering process involves not only a grasp of the first principles which govern the world, but also a comprehension of their complex and delicate balance and of the closeness of the false to the true.

IV

ﾟ

ARISTOTLE AND FORM

In introducing the characterization of metaphysics as "first philosophy," it has already been necessary to mention Aristotle's views and his special place in the history of metaphysics. Not only is it simply that this term is derived from the title given to those of his considerations which were "beyond physics," but also it is to Aristotle that we must attribute the beginning of a technical vocabulary for metaphysics. Other terms have been introduced, different stresses have been placed, and important revisions have been made in these definitions since his time; but any discussion of metaphysics still looks back to the technical terminology established by Aristotle.

Plato comes earlier in time, it is true, but the contrast between these two philosophers simply points up the two main ways of doing metaphysics. It highlights a choice which today still seems both open to us and subject to debate. That is, Plato is less formal in his arguments; he is less careful to give precise definitions, and apparently he is not as much interested in technical proof, but is more intent upon raising issues and offering a suggestive framework for their consideration. Aristotle, by contrast, introduces and defines technical terminology, and thus he outlines arguments more formally.

Not to see this basic difference in procedure is to miss one of the crucial choices to be made in approaching metaphysics, or else it is to decide the issue by default. Metaphysics means many things, and in approaching any one philosopher it is important to see how he conceived of this enterprise and the particular way in which he viewed what he expected to get from his own theory. We have already pointed out that Aristotle himself called this inquiry "first philosophy," and that he considered it an investigation of first principles which themselves were usually assumed as the basis for work in the sciences. Aristotle wanted to know if all Being could be considered, not in some special aspect or science, but simply as Being in general ("being *qua* being"), and he apparently thought that the general structures of all things could be defined. Our question is whether there is anything which is "simply first," something from which argument proceeds but which itself is not reducible to anything prior.

This need to establish a fixed beginning point is, as we shall see, both central and crucial to Aristotle's whole conception of philosophy, whereas Plato is more casual in his procedure and less concerned about the definiteness of limits. It is in metaphysics that the basic principles which characterize a particular view of philosophy are worked out. To neglect metaphysics may be to overlook the peculiarities of a philosophical approach or even to take philosophical procedure for granted, rather than to appraise critically one view of the function of philosophy as opposed to another. In Aristotle's case, the concept of *self-evidence* was particularly important to his understanding of philosophy and the function of metaphysics. In explaining situations, entities, events, or rules, we are always driven to account for them in terms of something else. It would seem, then, that there is no end to philosophical inquiry. This is something which Plato might have accepted, but to Aristotle this condition was a danger to the very possibility of assured knowledge. For Plato knowledge centered on the apprehension of Forms, but for Aristotle it seemed to involve the ability to set limits on inquiry and to reach a point of completion and rest.

"Self-evidence," however, does not always mean "obviousness," as the former term is sometimes taken to imply. This concept simply means that the explanation of a certain matter is not to be sought by examining something else, but can be discovered only within the thought itself. The evidence that accounts for the thing is contained in the thing itself and is not beyond it. The *law of noncontradiction* can be taken as a case in point. A thing cannot be both A and not-A at the same time and in the same way. This law cannot be made evident by reducing it to anything else or by calling other principles into play. If it is accepted, the evidence for its truth is self-contained; the truth is to be found by examining the concept of noncontradiction itself until its validity is established to the satisfaction of the inquirer. Metaphysics is just this search for principles which are *first*; first principles are to be referred to nothing beyond themselves for their proof. Instead, they are used as a basic starting point for further inquiry or deduction.

Aristotle does not insist that there can be only one such self-evident proposition or starting point for all Being (as do Descartes and Spinoza). In this sense, Aristotle's view has a great deal more flexibility than most theories, and it does not form one simple, neat system. Instead, Aristotle's metaphysics is the search for self-evident principles. Every philosopher begins by assuming that there is more than one such principle and that the metaphysician's task is to consider all such alternatives. Aristotle makes various suggestions as to the fixed points of reference by which he proposes to set the limits within which knowledge is possible, but metaphysics itself is regarded as simply the inquiry into such principles and not the formation of one tight theoretical view. The development of a full philosophy requires many other aspects—such as physics and psychology—but metaphysics is central to all inquiry. Metaphysics is a starting point, since it is the inquiry which aims at uncovering and examining the principles which are first because their evidence is contained within themselves.

In discussing Aristotle's conception of form, it is not our concern to comment on the similarities between Aristotle and Plato. We might expect to find areas of overlap between two major philosophers who are so close together in time, especially since Plato was Aristotle's teacher. In the interest of understanding metaphysics better, however, as we treat each figure we will concentrate on what is distinctive and different about the approach of each to metaphysics. The similarities between Plato and Aristotle, some of which are perplexing, have kept scholars busy for centuries. Yet to dwell on these areas of overlap would be to do something quite different from trying to see how a man's metaphysics gives his whole philosophical view a distinctive character. There is a technical meaning to metaphysics, as we have pointed out, but at least in this general sense it is important to understand metaphysics as the basic conception of the procedures and aims of philosophy itself. Some discipline must consider what philosophy is and what it ought to be. This kind of inquiry might be called "meta-philosophy" but, more traditionally, it is named "meta-physics."

A. Form and Category

If it is true that there are certain crucial terms, such as *form*, which occur and recur in metaphysical discussions, it should be clear that one way to understand metaphysics is to understand the way in which an author may give an old term a different meaning. In this way one comes to understand that the development of new metaphysical views is achieved by alterations of the meaning of concepts so that new aspects are highlighted. Aristotle agrees with Plato in making form central to knowledge, and he gives it many of the same properties: Form is universal and separable from the individual, it is unchanging in itself, and it is the source of the intelligibility in terms of which individual sense-objects are to be understood. As has often been noted, Aristotle's main disagreement with Plato comes over the existence and the status assigned to the forms of things. For Aristotle, forms do not exist as separable from the objects of the physical world, but exist only in them; they are extracted by human intelligence for the purpose of understanding.

Here it is important to note that Aristotle refuses to accept form as applying to such abstract properties as unity, for, after all, there are no sense-objects from which such a form could be abstracted. Plato was forced to propose his doctrine of the separate existence of the Forms in order to account for our knowledge of abstract concepts, but Aristotle is better able to limit the existence of forms simply to ingredients in the physical world because he does not attempt to include as forms properties other than those actually embodied in physical objects. Yet form does not stand alone for Aristotle; like most of his interpretative concepts, it is best understood by contrast with the concept which makes a pair with it. In this case, *matter* is understood together with *form,* and all objects are to be analyzed by the use of these two concepts. Matter is not something in itself, just as forms do not exist apart from actual objects; instead both matter and form are basic concepts in terms of which a variety of objects and instances may be grasped and analyzed.

Thus, what is form in one situation may become matter in another. Wood is the matter from which paper is made, but the form of the paper can in turn become the matter from which some design is cut. This type of analysis brings to mind Aristotle's famous doctrine of the *categories*, which achieve a new prominence and a quite different interpretation with Kant later on. There is an ultimate set of concepts in terms of which every object in the world may be classified and analyzed; this set is mutually exclusive and exhaustive of the basic concepts required for all understanding. *Essence, property,* and *accident* are the categories needed in terms of which the qualities of an object may be classified and grasped, and there is no possibility of reducing any of these to anything more basic. Rationality is *essential* to me as a man; humor is a *property* which accrues to me by virtue of being a man, but that I am presently in a ship on the Atlantic Ocean is an *accident* of my particular existence.

It is not so important to argue whether the categories of Aristotle are exhaustive of all the possible categories, or even whether he has defined them adequately. What is most important is to see the function of categories and to understand their purpose in metaphysics. Can we locate a set of irreducible concepts the grasp of which will give us a basis for the analysis and understanding of all possible objects? This is the question which is crucial to the very possibility of metaphysics. For if we want to grasp "being *qua* being," then we will need categories not applicable simply to some limited range of objects, but applicable to all possible objects. These concepts cannot be reducible to some further set, for they are the first principles of all analysis; they are mutually exclusive and evident simply by consideration of the internal meaning of the categories. For Aristotle, these categories are derived directly by abstraction from the physical world before us, and the task of abstraction is the chief function assigned to the mind. The categories form the firm limit which needs to be set for our minds and the ultimate reference point which is required if the quest for certain knowledge is to be achieved.

B. The Four Causes

Few philosophical concepts are more widely understood or more popularly known than Aristotle's famous division of all causes into four types: material, formal, efficient, and final. The first two, it is easy to see, are related to his analysis of all objects into matter and form. However, it is almost more important to understand

Aristotle's view of the centrality of *cause* in the achievement of knowledge. Grasping something with our senses, even if one is abstracting the forms which are present, is not enough to produce knowledge. We are said "to know" only when we have grasped the causes of the thing. If this is true, then we must know the various types of causes, so that in any instance we do not grasp one kind of cause and overlook some other crucial aspect. Aristotle argues that the causes, like the categories, form an exhaustive and irreducible set, and he contends that the four types of causes are mutually exclusive and complete.

The *material* cause of a thing is that from which the thing is made—either some physical material such as the cloth for a dress, or the words put together to form a speech. The *formal* cause is clearly the shape or structure given to the material—the pattern of the dress or the logic of the discourse. The *efficient* cause is the means by which the event is produced—the dressmaker who cuts the material or the rhetorical power of the speaker in marshaling his words.

The idea of a *final* cause is probably the most debated, but it is also perhaps the most important to Aristotle. This is not the place to discuss the teleology and purposiveness which Aristotle finds to be characteristic of all things, even in physical nature. In terms of metaphysics, a final cause—a goal or an aim—is just as important to Aristotle, in providing a base for understanding, as is a self-evident first principle. The intention to sell a dress for money, or the desire of a speaker to win an election—these are the sorts of final causes Aristotle speaks about, and they set the outside limit which is necessary in order to achieve knowledge, just as first principles offer a firm starting place for all analysis.

To explain fully, to criticize adequately, or to answer all the objections raised to Aristotle's concept of the four causes would require volumes, and actually it would not bring us any closer to our goal of understanding metaphysics. For to appraise the theory of the causes would not be a metaphysical inquiry but a critical one. What we want to grasp here is how the doctrine of the four causes gives us a fundamental way of understanding all things, and how, through the operation of causes, we learn the function and aim of all metaphysics. Such a grasp can provide us with understanding, whether or not we accept Aristotle's technical vocabulary and his rigorous and tightly-knit analysis. With this approach in mind, it is easy to see how the doctrine of the four causes fits together with his other metaphysical principles—such as the categories—to form a consistent

way of understanding nature. In a less systematic way, Plato's Forms
and "soul" operate together to complement each other as a basis for
understanding.

If knowledge must be limited in order to be achieved, then the
concept of the four causes helps to accomplish this limitation. Any
object in itself may lead on to an indefinite number of connections,
as Spinoza thinks it does. However, with the four causes, the way in
which we understand any event or object is given definite limits. The
causes explain all of a thing's aspects, but they do so only within a
set framework. This scheme makes reason's comprehensive grasp
possible precisely because the factors involved are definitely limited.
In this respect it is easy to note that, among the four, the final cause
stands as something of an exception to the others (just as Aristotle's
Unmoved Mover is important because it also is something of a special case among the class of movers); the final cause, far from being
limited, leads us beyond the object itself. This indefinite extension
involves relations which threaten the compact limitations upon
which knowledge depends. Any resolution to the problem of limitation will depend on Aristotle's ability to confine his whole system
without becoming involved in an indefinite regress. Thus, the concept of the four causes does not stand alone, but is dependent on
other metaphysical principles which Aristotle develops to support it.

C. Limit and Infinity

Perhaps there is nothing more characteristic of Aristotle's metaphysics or more important for understanding his approach than his
polemic against the existence of an actual infinite. What change
would the existence of an actual infinite require in Aristotle's first
principles, and how does he deal with this threat? It is sometimes
thought that the "transcendental" aspects of Plato's doctrine of the
Forms are the aspects which Aristotle rejects, but since Aristotle's
forms are very similar to Plato's, and his Unmoved Mover is transcendent in much the same sense in which the Forms are, it is hard
to place much weight on this argument. What seems much more
likely is that it is the very openness of Plato's process of knowledge
that bothers Aristotle most. There is a distinct sense in which Plato's
goal of knowledge is never fully achieved, and he is quite clear about
this where apprehension of the Good is concerned. Aristotle, on the
other hand, thinks that knowledge demands a process which can be

completed. Plato postulated the existence of his Forms in order to provide stable objects for knowledge. Aristotle's requirements are even stronger: The whole process must be both necessary and complete.

Reason, according to Aristotle's view, demands definiteness, and it is clear that to define is to set the limits of the thing. In thus demanding definiteness and a setting of limits, Aristotle objects to the modern attribute of "infinity"—as, say, a characteristic of God. In fact, it would never occur to him that God would be anything other than limited, and Aristotle's arguments for his Unmoved Mover rest on the necessity to set limits for all processes. Thus, the "proofs" of the existence of the Unmoved Mover are poor arguments for an infinite God (if they are used by someone who does not accept the need for limits in order to achieve knowledge). Aristotle's concern is to avoid an infinite regress of causes or an unending chain of inquiry in the attempt to understand. Every later philosopher who sets limits on the scope of the philosophical attempt is metaphysically akin to Aristotle, even if the methods which he uses to establish these limits are quite different from those of the author of *Metaphysics*. If philosophy is to fulfill a particular concept of itself, the first metaphysical decision involves determining the inquiry's need for limits.

Aristotle is well aware that it is impossible to remove every trace of infinity, so he settles on the compromise of infinity conceived of as existing only potentially and never as fully actual. Time runs on toward infinity, and in that sense time is infinite, although it is so only potentially and never as a completed whole. Any object or number is theoretically divisible to infinity, but the process is only potential and is never actually completed. In order to limit the infinite regress of causes, Aristotle uses the concept of the four causes. In a framework of the present time, this concept will allow all events to be analyzed into a rationally comprehensible form without continual extension backward.

Next, to provide a fixed point of reference to the process as a whole, the Unmoved Mover will be introduced; then, in order to give an explanation, the basic, self-evident first principles of this concept will form the basis of the movement of the argument. It is not that every item and aspect must be brought within this comprehension, for that might involve us in an infinity of detail. We are interested only in essence; therefore, much can be dropped out of our concern. This scope leaves only a small number of items to be grasped as necessary and as finite in number, and these principles compose an essential core of stable knowledge once they are set out.

We catch here perhaps *the* driving force behind Aristotle's thought, a question which metaphysics seeks to grasp and to consider: What must be true if knowledge is to be possible? Whenever we hear this basic question, as we will from Descartes and Kant, we know that metaphysical principles are being designed with epistemological ends in mind. Then, in order to appraise that particular metaphysics, the goals of knowledge and the priority of its requirements will have to be included. In a sense, Plato began with that question too, but either his ultimate view of knowledge was different or else he abandoned that question as a first consideration and became more interested in the first principles of all things for their own sake. It is true that Plato did have practical goals in mind, but there must be a difference in the degree of certainty each one feels is required in order to provide practical direction.

It may very well be that in the questions of the need for limit and the existence of infinity we have one of the key issues which underlies and shapes the direction of a metaphysics. If we do not set up limitation and completion as major goals, we are free to develop metaphysics and philosophy in more than one way. On the other hand, if we set a primary store on achieving certainty and assurance, our metaphysical principles and our basic philosophical approach will have to be geared accordingly. It is true that our decision on this matter has much to do with the way in which we conceive of the mind and its scope. Unfortunately, many begin with an initial assumption that the mind is equipped only for certain things and that it is restricted to a limited range. From an inspection of previous philosophies, we can see that there is no universal agreement about the mind's limitations. Thus, the range of the human mind ought not to be something simply assumed, but should be carefully worked out on the basis of the various possible alternatives open.

The question of the mind's powers is a matter which can be settled only by a theory of knowledge, but it is hard to know what the mind can and cannot grasp until we know the range and kind of objects open to us. Thus, many epistemologies begin with an initial assumption that the world presents us with only a few fundamental entities (for example, impressions and ideas, in Hume's case). The postulation of first principles is in itself a judgment of metaphysics; yet this postulation is absolutely crucial to the development of an epistemology, and it is equally important that we should test this assumption. Thus, a theory of knowledge cannot proceed without first describing the structure of the world about us, and the criticism of this characterization is metaphysics' job. Even if, as in the case of Kant, the assumption is that we cannot know things-in-themselves, but can only know appearances, this belief must not be assumed as self-evident until it is tested—and to do so is the task of metaphysics. For if the basic framework which is set is not without alternative, then it is important for the philosopher to be certain that he is not building an elaborate theory of knowledge on nothing more than an uncritical metaphysical assumption.

D. The Unmoved Mover

Aristotle's introduction of his concept of the Unmoved Mover at one point in his metaphysics is admittedly an important addition, but it has also been subject to criticism ever since. It is in our interest neither to get involved in the arguments supporting the existence of such a concept nor to appraise the criticism of this introduction as "unnecessary" or as involving needless complications. What we must understand is the place and function of this concept in Aristotle's thought. We must also understand what this idea tells us both about Aristotle's metaphysics and about other alternatives. Perhaps a study in contrasts between the Unmoved Mover and Plato's "soul" would be most instructive here. The Unmoved Mover causes motion without himself moving; he is pure actualized thought and thinks only upon himself. Aristotle fears motion more than Plato did, and Aristotle therefore finds it necessary to eliminate motion as an ultimate principle, since this concept is a block to intelligibility. Motion is fundamental, and yet Aristotle does not regard it as divine in the way that "soul" is for Plato.

Aristotle's preference for and stress upon the priority of *actuality* is important, and actuality has been regarded as equally important by countless thinkers since, although perhaps they did not need to go through so critical a process as Aristotle went through. Aristotle assigned the infinite a status as potential, and this should indicate potentiality's inferior role. His desire for definite limits and for completion dictated that actuality be made primary, and in this respect it can be seen that, given these assumptions, motion represents an incomplete and inferior state. Must motion be eliminated in order for thought to achieve its goal? It is clear that Plato does not think so but that Aristotle does. However, it is also clear that both have different views on the goal of knowledge and its requirements. Those who consider Aristotle's Unmoved Mover an unnecessary addition to his philosophy are probably much more Platonic than Aristotle was in their acceptance of motion as rational and ultimate, and they probably do not share Aristotle's goal to achieve knowledge by being able to set a limit to every unending process or tendency. The Unmoved Mover provides the limit on the world's unending series of causes.

Movement, then, for Aristotle, always indicates a lack and an incompletion. It is thus to be considered both an imperfection in a thing and a block to knowledge unless it is "stopped" by reference to something already completed which gives knowledge a motionless reference point. For Aristotle, rest is a more perfect state than motion, and desire is also an acknowledgment of an inferior status, whereas for Plato this is not the case. In classical theology it is sometimes thought that Plato's God was adopted by the dominant tradition, but those who say this are thinking only of the Forms and not of the central place which Plato gives to the self-motion of soul. Classical theology is much more apt to characterize God after the pattern of Aristotle's Unmoved Mover than after Plato's World Maker.

If Aristotle is the originator of metaphysics (as a technical enterprise), it is also true that he raises the question of the relation of theology to metaphysics, and he illustrates the function of God metaphysically. Aristotle's Unmoved Mover is not required religiously (perhaps it is not even religiously useful), but one can see reflected in the characteristics of his God the basic assumptions of Aristotle's metaphysics. If only one concept of God were possible, this situation would be quite different metaphysically, but this is not the case.

There seem to be at least as many gods as there are sets of basic metaphysical assumptions, so that God cannot simply be entered or deleted from a metaphysical scheme as a fixed concept. Rather, the concept of God reflects the total scheme into a focal point. Or, if a philosophical view has nothing like a concept of God, this tells us that the view is probably basically antimetaphysical (the views of Hume or even Kant, for example, versus those of Spinoza or Hegel). We understand the outlines of Aristotle's metaphysical principles and what they aim to achieve (limitation, completion, rationality by a fixed point of reference for all motion, and full actuality versus any potentiality). Aristotle's God exemplifies these goals. If we take different objects as metaphysically primary, we get either a different concept of God or, in some cases, no need for one at all.

V

❦

PLOTINUS AND TRANSCENDENCE

The distinctive features of Plotinus's metaphysics are often thought to have come from Plato. There are reasons which account for this important confusion—namely, the loss of Plato's dialogues for centuries, and Augustine's use of Plotinus while simply referring to his thought as "Platonistic"—but it is not relevant here to trace out those complicated stories. What we want to see is whether we can discover the distinctive features of Plotinus's first principles which set him quite far apart from Plato, whatever the affinities between the two may be. It is true that Plotinus often forms his views by commenting on Plato's dialogues, but such closeness of thought ought only to teach us that the use of another man's theories may actually generate a quite different basic outlook. This is certainly true of Aristotle's use of Plato and, as we shall see, of Kierkegaard's protest against Hegel. What did Plotinus take over from Plato, and in what way does the new stress which he gives to their common problems lead him to a different doctrine?

A. The Demand for Unity

The centrality which Plotinus gives to the demands of *unity* is crucial to our understanding here. The requirements involved in

55

making unity a dominant concept ultimately led Plotinus to a wide divergence from the principles of Platonic thought. In considering the doctrines of Parmenides in Plato's dialogue bearing that name, Plato traced out quite clearly the consequences of the demand for absolute unity—namely, the complete dominance of the One without any second attribute. Plato actually rejects this extreme, and he traces out a complex involvement of the One with the Many. He seems to recommend a compromise between the two principles in proposing the rule of "definite number."

Plotinus, however, reverses Plato and endorses the demands for unqualified unity as a metaphysical rule, and he then traces out the far-reaching consequences of this first principle. The Platonic compromise forced Plato to adopt a view of unity as being slightly unstable. For him, unity tends to move either toward greater simplicity or toward increasing multiplicity whenever the soul and its reasoning powers are not constantly on guard to maintain balance. Plotinus rejects this uneasy compromise. Such continual instability is unacceptable to him, and he stresses the crucial role of increasing simplicity. In the hierarchy of concepts, the One becomes dominant.

The difference between Plato and Plotinus may be seen most clearly if one compares the multiplicity and essential difference in kind of the Platonic first principles with Plotinus's single principle on which all else depends: The One. "Soul," "Forms," the "receptacle" or random motion and chaos, the "Good," and perhaps "reason"—for Plato all these remain basic principles which are irreducible to any single concept. Such ultimate multiplicity is unacceptable to Plotinus, and as a result he produces a much different basis for metaphysics. Obviously, to do so involves the difficult task of trying to explain how one first principle can give rise to an account for qualities and kinds of Being which apparently are so different from it. This becomes Plotinus's chief problem, whereas Plato's multiplicity of first principles makes it easier for him to account for a wide variety of forms of life. Yet the virtues of a single and supreme metaphysical principle are important too. We can see what these are by contrasting a single principle with the loose-knit Aristotelian principles, which many deny can ever be put together into what can be called a systematic metaphysics. Individual problems can be analyzed, but for Aristotle no unity obtains among all of the principles.

Clearly the centrality of the Christian God in any scheme of things owes more to a basic Plotinian outlook than to the views of

Plato or Aristotle. Aristotle's argument for the need of an Unmoved Mover as a focal point for knowledge—which seeks limitation and completion—obviously leads to the Unmoved Mover as simply one principle among many, not to a transcendent single principle. Such unity of first principles is the characteristic of Plotinus, and this singularity becomes central for Christian theology.

Reason, for Plato, seeks to discern and to articulate the Many in the One and the One in the Many. For Plotinus, on the other hand, reason is given a quite different goal and a new status, just as a different view of reason's requirements leads Aristotle to demand limitedness and completion as his chief goals in knowledge. Plotinian reason primarily seeks increasing unity and simplicity among the multiple events. For Plotinus, reason's direction is singular, not double as it is for Plato's philosopher, who must at the same time combine an abstract speculative grasp with the mundane interests of a king. If the search for unity now demands it, Aristotle's prized limitation in order to achieve completion will have to be abandoned too. Reason has a new goal, and, in its quest for absolute unity, all limitations are broken, and even certainty is abandoned.

B. Beyond Intelligence

Kant and Hume both developed a critique of reason's ability; but at an earlier date, and perhaps in a more drastic way, Plotinus had already accomplished that task. According to Plotinus, reason alone is inadequate to provide the ultimate unity of all things that is demanded. Those who take reason as supreme and as never to be violated assume uncritically some ultimate status for reason, and an examination of the nature of things may or may not support this. Reason, at least for Plotinus, is only to be understood by reference to that from which it flows and that toward which it is oriented. The same is true of Plato and Aristotle, except that the "genealogy" which Plato traces out for reason is different, and Aristotle's jealousy over the demands of reason is more ultimate. It is well known that for Plotinus reason as a principle occupies only a second position in the hierarchy of things and is not even to be taken as ultimate in that position. Since Plotinus desires one first principle rather than many, in this case reason must be subordinated and understood in its position beneath the One.

Soul had a certain ultimacy as an explanatory principle for Plato.

For Plotinus, however, soul is placed third on the ladder. Soul is simply reason's embodiment as it moves away from the One, and physical bodies are simply that side of the individual soul which appear as it is turned even further away from reason and from the One which is beyond it. Such a hierarchy—One, Reason, and Soul, together with the physical tendency to extreme multiplicity beyond that—is easy to grasp, and it gives an order and a neatness in our approach to the world which neither Plato nor Aristotle can match.

It is no wonder that Plotinus's metaphysical triad did and still does have powerful appeal for all those who prize simplicity in explanation, particularly in religious and theological circles. Those thinkers who fight against any tendency toward transcendence will miss the clean, clear, and invigorating refreshment which comes from such singleness of direction. Perhaps those thinkers exalt reason too much without inquiring into its possible secondary and dependent status. When unity and simplicity are given full sway as first principles in metaphysics, nothing can be left standing which thwarts that goal, not even reason itself.

Yet, why is it that reason (even Reason as a principle) must be transcended in the name of the One? Clearly, reasoning ordinarily involves discursive movement and thus multiplicity. Even in its ultimate development—in Aristotle's Unmoved Mover's contemplation of thought thinking on itself—there must always be at least the division between thought and its object. For one who seeks unbroken unity, any potential source of division is a peril. The presence of division indicates a failure to reach the ultimate principle and shows that we are still, at best, on a secondary level in our search for metaphysical first principles. And why is any division, even that between thought and its object, such a danger? Because Aristotle knew that anything which is even potentially divisible is actually divisible *ad infinitum*. Thus, in the presence of any distinction there lurks the tendency to an increased multiplicity, and this indicates that our goal lies in another direction. However, reason is ranked just beneath the principle of unity, and reason leads to unity because it exemplifies unity better than does any other principle in the world's structure. By its nature reason always seeks to reduce multiplicity to unity. Plotinus denies that Plato's inclusion of the opposite direction is good; that is, although reason does move toward multiplicity naturally, for Plotinus this tendency is away from good and toward evil.

Thought is not present within Plotinus's first principle except insofar as the One is turned downward to consider the orders below it. In itself all thought must come to rest, and it must do so in a more drastic fashion than Aristotle ever demanded. Thought is necessary only if we want to deal with division and multiplicity. It is an instrument called forth by the practical necessities of living on a level lower than the highest. Wherever unity is perfect, thought is unnecessary. Thus, transcending reason is lamented only by those who do not realize that it is no longer needed. Plotinus often calls his first principle the *Good*, which makes it reminiscent of Plato's concept. This term indicates the value direction that is implicit in Plotinus's unrelenting quest for both greater simplicity and increasing degrees of unity. In the direction of unity and simplicity lies all that is good, even the source of all the many levels of things which are less ultimate in their mode of existence. Away from unity and toward increasing multiplicity and division—it is this direction that ultimately produces evil. The ethical implications of this line of reasoning should be easy to discern; unity is associated with purity, and multiplicity with corruption.

In spite of the lower statuses which he gives to both soul and reason in relation to the One as the first principle, it is interesting to see Plotinus's great sensitivity to psychological modes. In fact, the sensitivity to interior states which we associate with the source of Augustine's metaphysics undoubtedly has some of its origins in Plotinus's acute observations. It is in his analysis of the human soul that Plotinus first uncovers his basic norm of simplicity and unity as the ultimate goal of thought, and as thought's governing principle. The soul is less divisible than the body, Plotinus observes, for when a leg is lost we do not think of a certain percent of the soul as being gone too. The soul also reacts more as a unified entity than does the body, which has more diverse and multiple functions. Reason is thought of as a principle which directs the soul's function as a unity, and its activity can draw the soul toward greater unity than it can if the soul moves away from reason's guidance and is attached to the body's more multiple ambitions. Thus a hierarchy is discovered within the soul's psychological activities, but, as we have seen, reason is not itself the pure example of the unity which it appears to be in its relation both to the physical body and to the diverse world around it.

Therefore, there is a desire to resolve the emotional tensions of the psychic life and to guide the soul among the fantastic demands of the multiple world which it tears itself apart trying to satisfy. The norm of unity and simplicity is found in this psychological quest.

The way first leads up through reason to greater unity and then down through the body to greater divisions and toward unending multiplicity. Plato advocated a strong stand at the center which would hold both tendencies together by force, but Plotinus has adopted a single goal and thus a single first principle. If followed to its logical conclusion, that goal ultimately leads beyond reason. Those who have not seen the constant danger and tendency toward evil which lies in multiplicity will lament this transcendence as a loss. Those who have awakened to a purified vision of the soul's source will celebrate transcendence as a return home and as a welcome relief from a burden which is inescapable in itself. This fact seems to be verified in the history of our lack of harmony and agreement over what reason is and does.

C. Good and Evil

It ought to be abundantly clear by now that what the problems of metaphysics are depends upon the conception a particular metaphysics has of its task. That is why we show a lack of sophistication and a failure to become sensitive to the complexities of the enterprise if we hold every metaphysics responsible for providing a solution to every problem. We must also see the weaknesses implicit in any proposed solution. Plotinus achieves the simplicity of a single first principle and the clarity of having only one direction for the attention of any man who seeks wisdom. However, according to his view, reason becomes a means and not an end. This circumstance provides a clear key to the solution when it is understood, but nevertheless reason is something which must be abandoned in the end for the next goal toward which it points, namely, unity. Reason embodies this end to a high degree but still only imperfectly. Plato "transcends" the sense world to a degree, but only in order to illuminate it and to hold it in better balance. Aristotle achieves his goal of knowledge by setting limits, but his account covers only an essential core and not all things. Plotinus advocates the return to the comprehensive goal of tracing all things to one source, but of necessity his direction must lead continually away from the multiplicity which he sought to explain.

Nowhere are the assets and the liabilities (the "problems") of Plotinus's metaphysical view more apparent than in the resulting statuses assigned to good and evil. Aristotle eliminated ethics from the central systematic concern of metaphysics. Presumably he did this in order to narrow the range for the achievement of knowledge, although his metaphysical principles can be seen as reflected in some of his ethical doctrine. Plato's principles are more fluid, and he sees ethics as being involved in every philosophical quest for understanding; hence he writes, "Knowledge is virtue." With Plotinus, value considerations are really spread across the map of metaphysical concern, so that those who later talk about a "hierarchy of values" have Plotinus as their metaphysical godfather. "Good" is the second name Plotinus gives to his first principle, the One, and the two terms are said to indicate one thing. Now it is easy to see that the soul's virtue—indeed its salvation—lies in locating and in achieving ever greater degrees of unity and simplicity. In fact, the soul must abandon even the self, if that proves necessary, in the pursuit of this supreme value.

That which promotes unity and simplicity becomes good, and the opposite tendency toward division and multiplicity is the road to increasing evil. The soul seeks to purify itself and to detach itself from the physical multiplicities which threaten to divide it. It strives to attach itself to its ultimate source, and this is to be achieved by greater participation in reason until finally even reason is surmounted. Every mystical and contemplative religious order owes to Plotinus's mystical vision as much as or more than it does to Jesus's vision of himself as a "suffering servant." "Good," however, is not a problem on this account. Even if one might prefer Plato's identification of good with the well-mixed life, there are no difficulties involved in pursuing Plotinus's Good if the nature of the principle and the transcendental consequences of this quest are acceptable.

Evil itself, however, is a more difficult problem. In some sense it is clear that all tendencies toward unmanageable multiplicity and division—as in a split personality—are bad and are to be avoided. But the description of the soul as being lower than reason, and that of all physical existence as sharing even more in the tendency to evil—such a characterization does not always seem to be fair to the attractiveness of the physical world. To be sure, in addition to a perceptive psychology, Plotinus had a fully developed esthetic theory, and he was well aware that beauty appears in sensuous objects all about us. It is just that for Plotinus this visible beauty must be seen as derivative from the nonsensible unity which is present in the object. The presence of unity in physical objects is not itself a product of the multiplicity of the world, but rather it is the reflection in the lower realms of the presence of a higher order. This view is still common in the esthetic interpretation of art. Thus, the world is by no means devoid of beauty and pleasures, but, in the sense that they are good, both beauty and pleasure lead beyond their physical presence and attract the soul toward achieving a higher existence. The soul is attracted even at the expense of abandoning its present life.

Since we grant that the world, then, is not falsely labeled as "evil," what is "the problem of evil" which results from adopting Plotinus's metaphysical principles? It is that evil must be considered as depending on the degree of distance from the One. Evil is a lack and a deficiency of Being, since the One, together with our nearness to it, is the source of all power. As Augustine and much of the Christian tradition come to say, evil is not a positive quality; it is nothing but a lack, a deficiency, an absence, a matter of distance from the source of Being, a tendency toward multiplicity and away from the center.

Since we grant that some evil seems to be negative and that this view saves us the difficulty of a split in the source of power in Being itself (since the Good is the only source of all power of existence), is this view sufficient to account for the positive and powerful destructive force which evil seems, at least at times, to exert? Furthermore, although the Good can be said to be "diffusive of itself"—"ungrudging" in communicating its power, as Plato would say—what explains its initial downward tendency toward evil in the first place? That good should be communicated in various degrees to all the other levels of existence, this seems easy enough to understand, but any tendency toward evil and destruction is itself left essentially unexplained. There cannot be a "reason" for the existence of this downward movement because of the way in which Plotinus has arranged his principles. Evil's presence remains a mystery, and this fact cannot be otherwise.

The direction toward the Good is the opposite of the downward tendency toward evil. Thus, such a theory is the opposite of Christian "incarnation," which views God as a servant of the lowly. Therefore, if we follow Plotinus's recommendations, we "escape" from the problem of evil, since the problem diminishes as the progress upward toward the One increases. But to escape from a problem is not the same as to resolve it, and, within a Plotinian framework, to give a rational account of the presence of evil and its positive power is, in the nature of the case, incompatible with his basic principles. The only thing for Plotinus to do with evil is to leave its force and its positive presence unexplained.

D. The Problem of the Lower Orders

Almost more unresolvable than the problem of explaining evil's positive presence is our inability—which Plotinus freely admits—to give an explanation of why anything at all has existence. The One certainly has no need of anything else, not even existence, particularly for anything lower than itself on the scale of degree of ontological value. The creation of orders which are beneath the One, even reason, involves the creation of something inferior. The existence of these orders implies a movement constantly downward, away from unity and toward what ultimately can only be pure Nonbeing or evil. Why should the One move in this direction in creation at all, since it is contrary to the habitual direction toward unity? In creation, the One seems to succeed only in producing even more inferior Goods, and these tend to move as much away from Being's source as toward it. The answer is that we cannot account for the creation of such inferior ranks. By looking about us we can see that all things must have flowed out of the Good, and all we can do is accept that as a fact. We do know that no rational decision could prompt creation, since the One has no need to reason, and thus nothing could be withheld in any creation. All kinds and every order and mode of Being must flow from the One out to the very limits of possibility— toward absolute Nonbeing. The One is so "full" that it unconsciously communicates itself and flows outward without thought or intention.

Although no ultimate reason can be given for our level of existence, we know that our created order is as full as it could be, since no possibility could fail to come forth in this tendency toward indefinite multiplicity. Now that a created hierarchical order is here, we may retrace its path. It is true that the order is eternal in its origin, since no reason could be given as to why the created order was brought forth at one time rather than another (a principle which seems to restrict Thomas Aquinas's Christian God too). The reason for the existence of any given entity can no more be stated conclusively than the form of the whole can be explained, but certainly this must be the only possible world. All we can say is that the fullness of Being required each part, so that nothing is neglected which could possibly come forth. The One, of course, in some sense must contain all the multiplicity which flows from it, but it does so without separation or distinction; it does not think about creating multiplicities.

Although we can neither reason about why there is a created

order at all nor understand the presence of any individual other than by its place in the whole, we do learn something from our inability to explain the "going forth." That is, we see the true direction which the labors of our reason should follow. Since the One has no need to reason, it does not and could not attempt to "explain" its purposes. To learn the fruitlessness of tracing out the way down from the One is perhaps also to learn our true path by recalling true divinity. The only successful direction for reason's effort is toward a reunion with its sources, sources which are also ours. Reason's intelligible motion does not seek an explanation of multiplicity, for there is none. It seeks increased unity and, ultimately, an identity with it. It does not follow, as some have thought, that our present level of existence is meaningless. However, the absence of explanation does mean that, on Plotinus's terms, existence cannot be made intelligible on its own. The reason for the existence of any entity is to be discovered in the search for its origin in a principle which is not like it in kind, but which is more nearly divine—namely, the One.

Thus, Plotinus's metaphysical view has a distinctively ethical flavor, one which bears the implications of a moral quest. A metaphysician does not abstractly postulate first principles and then construct explanations on the basis of them. Or, if he begins that way, to the extent that he fathoms the principles which govern and arrange all Being, he will sense Being's direction and see the status of the soul, his own included, in this hierarchical order. He should be moved by this vision to turn the direction of his own soul from evil to good. When Aristotle discovers the virtue which the Unmoved Mover has of putting a limit on the otherwise unending tendencies of knowledge that would destroy its achievement, he can and does recommend that men seek to imitate the life of the Unmoved Mover. Plato thinks that the guidance of a rational and yet inspired soul is a good thing, but neither of these men can match the strong ethical and almost religious quest which always seems to be involved in the discovery of Plotinus's first principles, or rather in learning the fact that there really is only One.

E. The Point of No Return

In helping us to understanding the possibilities of metaphysics, Plotinus has one important contribution to make: He calls the whole enterprise itself into question. He does this not, as some might do, by questioning the possibility of metaphysics or by complaining that one cannot be certain of its truth, but rather by suggesting that perhaps metaphysics is not enough to have as philosophy's basic goal. Metaphysics is defined by Aristotle's question as to whether it is possible to go beyond (*meta*) the individual concerns of a science (physics) in order to inquire about the first principles which apply not simply to one area of Being, but to all of it. Aristotle gives a positive answer to this question, and Plato's suggestions can also be fitted into this framework, in spite of the difference between the two men. In inquiring about the soul and its relation to the body and its reasoning capacity, Plotinus certainly begins with the same inquiry into the origin and structure of Being. The point is that he does not stay within even those ambitious bounds.

In all of Being that is good, Plotinus detects this tendency toward one direction, and then a "point of no return" is passed. That is, we no longer want simply to account for the structure of all Being, but we now want to pass beyond it ourselves by losing our individual and separated selves. Sensing that the operating principle is unity as it accounts for the levels of diversity, we next discover that the true goal is to pass beyond all structure, since even reason is an imperfect representation of the principle which actually animates all Being. Except for Plato's slight hint of transcendence in the case of the Good (a point not unconnected with the direction in which Plotinian doctrine moves), both Plato and Aristotle were content to accept the account of Being's structure as philosophy's ultimate goal. Plato detected the transcendental tendencies in the complete dominance of the concept of unity as an uncompromising principle in his dialogue *Parmenides*, and he rejected this in favor of a compromise that accepts our present varied structure as being ultimate. By contrast, it is Plotinus's discovery about the basic structure of Being that leads him to reject it as ultimate. *Meta*-physics is no longer enough, and reason must now reach silence if it is to discover its final source.

The clear single direction which we discover in Plotinus is perhaps the best contrasting background against which to sort out all of metaphysics' problems. More sharply than perhaps any other philosopher, Plotinus raises the question of the aim of metaphysics, and he points out the issue—which must be dealt with—of its relation to ethical goals and to theology. For instance, if Plato's World Maker must look both to the immutable Platonic Forms and to the created order still in chaos, Aristotle's Unmoved Mover creates by no action of his own and looks only to himself, which is the line of vision of

Aquinas's God too. Plotinus's God, however, does not look down at all. In fact, he is not even a God in the usual sense, because the possession of feeling and even reason would involve him in inferiority. The One is a principle ordering all things in descending levels, and thus it draws us up toward its own level just to the degree that the principle operating in us is fully clarified and recovered. This is reason's aim—to surpass itself.

The theological implications of these three schemes make clear the importance of being fully aware of the variety of directions open to us in deciding about the problems of metaphysics. The status and role assigned to metaphysics are matters of importance, since the shape theology can and will take is also at stake. With Plato, Aristotle, and Plotinus the goal and the function of knowledge are themselves very much issues. For Plato and for Aristotle, although in differing ways, metaphysics seems to be called for either to support the goal of knowledge (Plato) or to provide the limiting principles necessary to achieve it (Aristotle). With Plotinus, knowledge seems to be assigned a subordinate place due to the discovery that Being's ultimate principle is unity.

Thus, although we cannot simply say that a theory of knowledge always results from the metaphysics which is developed, as does a view of God's nature, still it is true that epistemology and metaphysics are coordinated enterprises. Each is worked out in the development of the other. This is no less true for those who, for the sake of knowledge, would restrict metaphysics (Kant) or even reject it (Hume). A basic view of the world becomes no less clearly visible in the course of explaining why the claims of knowledge either restrict or inhibit metaphysical inquiry. One of the first problems of metaphysics, Plotinus teaches us, is to determine how the procedures and goals of knowledge are to be defined and, more than that, whether knowledge itself is even our ultimate goal.

VI

DESCARTES
AND CERTAINTY

From Plotinus we pass right over the whole of the Middle Ages to the beginning of modern philosophy, for our aim is not to give a comprehensive history of metaphysics, but to provide a fresh understanding of its problems. Still, why pass over the Middle Ages? Was medieval philosophy not metaphysical? After all, because of the close involvement of philosophy with theology during the Middle Ages, the medieval period was perhaps the most uniformly metaphysical age in philosophy's history. And was not medieval philosophy novel in its contributions to the enterprise of metaphysics? Instead of answering these questions, we will bypass this complicated issue and simply assert that, for an understanding of metaphysics today, the changes which came about at the end of the union of theology and philosophy are presently the most crucial for us, especially since metaphysics is now enjoying a creative revival.

A. Modern Metaphysics

You will note that our argument above has nothing to do with proposing that we abandon classical metaphysics. On the contrary, we have spent the last three chapters tracing out the essentials of three influential classical theories. It is a commonplace to say that metaphysics as an enterprise has been under attack in recent times. Actually, it is probably more accurate to say that there never has been a time when metaphysics was not under attack. Since no single metaphysical scheme has been fixed for us, there will always be a rivalry between different views. Furthermore, both philosophers and nonphilosophers have always been skeptical of schemes which involve the maximum generality, which metaphysical views do of necessity. Nevertheless, modern philosophy did develop special concerns which have given a slant to all of metaphysics in our era. Thus, in order to see metaphysical problems clearly today, it is first necessary to fight our way free from accepting any given approach as being ultimate. The three opening chapters were an attempt to set out metaphysics as it was and not as it came to be reinterpreted in a later day. In understanding metaphysics, it is absolutely crucial that no single framework for interpretation be taken as ultimate.

If the first business of metaphysics is the comparison of various sets of first principles, then from this fact we learn something important about any attacks which are made against metaphysics, and also something crucial for the construction of a metaphysical theory. That is, if all metaphysical schemes do not have the same bases or conceptions of themselves or of their procudures, then it is simply impossible to argue against all metaphysics at once. It usually is true that antimetaphysical reactions have arisen against some one view— for example, British Positivism and Linguistic Analysis against one form of Idealism, and Kierkegaard against one understanding of Hegel. Yet, for some strange reason, each reaction seems to treat the particular view against which it reacts as if it were in itself all of metaphysics, or at least each attack appears to assume that the way in which some one objectionable view phrases its task in certain peculiar technical terms is the only way of formulating the problems of metaphysics. Perhaps this is a left-handed compliment to the metaphysician who is under attack, in that he seems to have convinced at least his attackers that his is *the way* to express and do metaphysics.

It is always more difficult to hit a moving target, so all criticism, whether metaphysical or otherwise, seems to have to freeze its moving target at some point and in some one form in order to mount an attack. This artificial procedure is perhaps necessary to the critical activity, but for the metaphysician it is equally necessary to see that the actual situation is nowhere near that simple or clear. Yet, just as it is impossible to destroy metaphysics without adopting some one position about the nature and function of philosophy which in turn may be objected to, and then fixing metaphysics in some one view (as with Hegel), so also it is impossible to do metaphysics by taking in at one time all that has been or can be. To study a wide variety of views has a liberating effect, and this procedure may also be a necessary introduction to metaphysics. However, when the constructive task begins, gradually one view of philosophy's nature and task will emerge, and one context of principles will begin to form within which a metaphysical interpretation is to be shaped.

An objection to some one doctrine is not the only thing which metaphysics has to fear. As its history has illustrated, an attack on one metaphysical approach usually leads to the formation of an alternative set of first principles. If this is not done explicitly, at least it comes about implicitly, as in the work of Kierkegaard and Hegel. An attack on any particular form of metaphysics usually leads to the inauguration of a metaphysical age. Positivism has led to a current metaphysical rebirth in England, because it is impossible to mount an antimetaphysical attack without developing your own first principles (and hence, a metaphysics) which undergirds the critical argument. If these implicit metaphysical assumptions are not clear at first, they soon become so in the course of debate. Then the very conception of philosophy itself comes up for discussion, and little can be more conducive to the investigation of first principles than this basic reexamination. As we began by saying, philosophy is that enterprise whose first question is always itself. Thus, whenever philosophy itself is actively under debate, we are sensitive to its basic nature and are inclined toward the examination of first principles and, thus, toward developing a metaphysics.

What follows from this is that all that is really dangerous to metaphysics is an uncritical dogmatism about the nature of philosophy, as, for instance, when a philosopher takes his way of analyzing things to be the only possible way and does not attempt to justify it or to consider alternatives. It is possible, but never obvious, that philosophy's only task is to investigate and to clarify various forms of linguistic expression. Such a view, or any other one, for that matter, is not in itself detrimental to metaphysics as a basic enterprise as long as the definition of the philosophical task and its procedures are not themselves taken as a closed or as an obvious matter.

As long as any given conception of philosophy is itself admitted to be open to debate and subject to basic challenge, however fruitful or attractive it may be in itself, metaphysics as a basic enterprise is never in danger. This security holds true even if one particular formulation of what philosophy's task is should turn out to be opposed to a certain type of metaphysics. If opposition to one form of metaphysics gives rise to a new view of the nature of philosophy itself, that is a direct compliment to the power of metaphysics, and the criticism becomes, in fact, a metaphysical enterprise itself.

B. The Quest for Certainty

When a particular metaphysical view is under attack in any given day, then it is a good idea to go back to an earlier era in order to get a contrasting idea of what metaphysics has been and might be. By doing this you can hope to avoid identifying all of metaphysics with some one current formulation. Whenever metaphysics has been revived, this type of backtracking has often taken place. That is, we go back to an earlier era and recover an idea for philosophical procedure which bypasses some particular form of philosophy that clearly is deadlocked at present. Thus, in the remaining chapters, we will begin to do less and less of the type of simple exposition of individual views that we did with Plato, Aristotle, and Plotinus. From now on, we will combine the exposition of the peculiar outlook on metaphysics of each man with a more critical and comparative attempt to understand what metaphysical problems are, and the various ways in which they can be dealt with.

Metaphysics is not simply the history of philosophy, and to do metaphysics is not simply to expound certain views. Rather, metaphysics has always involved understanding a basic context for philosophy—Descartes in this case—while at the same time reacting against that context critically. Our hope is to find a new direction from this study and not simply to repeat the direction which another man found by the same exploration in his own earlier day. *There simply is no way to understand metaphysics neutrally, even historically, without engaging in its construction.*

Descartes is quite clear about the fact that his view of philosophy involves a quest for certainty, and some thinkers—for example, John Dewey—have thought that this same goal characterizes all metaphysics. We will not attempt to go into the reasons which compelled Descartes to identify philosophy with the necessity for achieving certainty, or even why he thought that achieving certainty was necessary. What we must do is examine this quest for certainty as a metaphysical goal which has at least colored, if not dominated, most modern approaches to metaphysics. If it is clear that Descartes had science and mathematics in mind as his models, then the following questions are raised: Does science unavoidably conceive of itself as seeking necessity and certainty in its theories? What relation ought philosophy to have to physical science as an enterprise? Must there be an identity of goals and procedures between philosophy and mathematics and science? Although it does seem clear that both science and mathematics have changed their views of themselves quite radically (which, if true, would leave Cartesian metaphysics pursuing an antique science), it is not our intention to try to answer these questions. In the spirit of metaphysics, we want to probe and uncover the assumptions which underlie this view. In the case of Descartes, it is important to question his goal of certainty before going on to criticize either his procedures or the validity of the arguments which he gives.

Almost nowhere before in the history of philosophy has the desire to obtain certainty in the propositions of philosophy been so strong as it is in Descartes's thinking. Certainly Plato cannot be identified with this goal, since he thought truth could not be communicated directly in written words. Thus, according to Plato, we must use only indirect techniques in presenting our theories—for example, by writing dialogues. True, the Platonic Forms are eternal and immutable, and they are a necessary stable reference point for knowledge, but it does not at all follow that man may formulate Plato's verbal or written philosophy so that it, too, becomes eternal and immutable. In fact, to be a Platonic philosopher is, in the nature of the case, to be committed to accepting a continued "existence in midair." We are always aware of a greater certainty, and we can approximate it more than an animal or an unreflective person might, but we are also always denied its final attainment.

Plotinus, who had a willingness to transcend even reason in the pursuit of the desirable consequences of pure unity, did not even come close to obtaining certainty as his reward. "Certainty" applies to propositions and to our thoughts about them, but for Plotinus this had to be abandoned at a crucial stage of metaphysical inquiry. Aristotle, on the other hand, did want at least a core of certainty and necessity, but he knew that philosophy must be limited in its scope if achieving this goal is to be made possible, and for this reason much in philosophy—for example, ethics and politics—can never reach certainty. Aristotle, then, shared some of Descartes's aspirations for philosophy, but Descartes gives this love of certainty a new and an unequivocal form, a form which embraces philosophy as a whole enterprise and thus requires the separation of philosophy from the uncertainty inherent in theology. Furthermore, Descartes places this goal on a ground quite different from Aristotle's basic principles. That is, Descartes's work is founded on a knowledge that begins in self-meditation and in the search for the one indubitable proposition that could serve as a touchstone for all of philosophy. That proposition is: "I think, therefore I am."

C. Self-Evident Propositions

We need to ask whether modern scientific theory demands of philosophy that it have a basis in certainty in order to insure its respectability, and we must also ask whether metaphysics can still pursue its aims in another form if this strict goal is abandoned. Descartes, and other moderns too, thought that the constant rivalry between alternative metaphysical views was a disgrace, and that the inability of metaphysicians to come to a final common decision was an intolerable situation. Yet Descartes's conclusion rests on a view of philosophy's nature and task which must be questioned carefully before it can be accepted.

Perhaps the world of theory is not subject to such finalization in any realm. More important, it could be that our world and its origin is such that no theory about it, however suggestive, can hope to be final (as Plato told us in the *Timaeus*, no account can be more than a "likely tale"). To condemn philosophy for failing to assume that its goal is already established is to misunderstand philosophy's function. Metaphysics should begin by trying to reach clarity on the nature of philosophy, its procedures and its aims. If philosophy itself cannot establish a final formulation of its own nature—a formulation which is beyond dispute and which is invulnerable to any possible future rejection—then in that sense its task is never completed. Each individual philosopher may succeed in achieving his goals within a given assumed context, but that context is exactly what other philosophers never take for granted. The next new philosophy begins by challenging the assumptions which the one before it took for granted.

Our fundamental questions about Descartes and his search for a single self-evident proposition—a statement which would be so clearly indubitable that no man could deny it, and thus one which could serve as a basis and example for all philosophical thought—concern the status of propositions themselves. Descartes seems to operate on an assumption that propositions are the real stuff of philosophy and that they are in some sense self-contained. On the other hand, to concentrate on thoughts and the propositions which express them may be to direct our attention to something which has only a secondary and derivative mode of existence. To question this procedure is not only important but crucial.

If, as both Plato and Aristotle thought, the mind actually gains all of its knowledge from an apprehension of objects, then it is to these objects that the mind should direct itself and not simply to either thought or propositions. Descartes, of course, has a different theory about the mind's relation to objects, but in metaphysics it is our business to question this assumption, although it may also be Descartes's business to explore fully the consequences of his basic assumption.

In other words, even if Descartes is convinced that the mere fact that he thinks and doubts can in itself establish his existence beyond doubt, we still must ask what such a self-evident proposition can do for philosophy, even if it is accepted. As we have seen, Aristotle considered it metaphysics' business to seek self-evident premises—assumptions so basic that their evidence could be obtained only by considering them and not by referring them to any assumptions more basic. Descartes's famous "I think, therefore I am" certainly is metaphysical in this sense, but Aristotle also seemed to be aware that there might be more than one such certain and indubitable proposition.

Philosophy is not grounded once and for all when one premise is reached that can only be analyzed internally for its evidence. Rather, metaphysics begins at that point with the comparison and contrast of this premise with other possible first principles. Descartes had hoped that only one such proposition would be possible, and that, once it was discovered, his quest for certainty would be over. However, if metaphysics' task is to achieve a comparison between alternative starting points, it certainly follows that there is no one proposition which can be assumed with certainty. Whatever the interesting qualities and consequences of a proposition may be, nothing forces us to begin at that point.

As we will see, Descartes followed Aristotle in restricting the scope of philosophy in order to accomplish his goal of certainty. Yet Aristotle seemed to know that his restriction of philosophy was itself open to question, whereas Descartes and other moderns appear more provincial in assuming that everyone else will agree with their limitation of philosophy to one form and starting point. The history of the treatment of Descartes's ideas indicates that he did indeed formulate a proposition which is evident either through itself or in no other way. Thus, Descartes's claim is basically metaphysical, but history also indicates that immediately after he uttered it, a challenge was made to his very starting point. In this sense Descartes has been helpful to metaphysics, for he raised the question of the starting point for philosophy itself.

All of us in the modern period come back to Descartes because he suggested that the new origin of philosophical inquiry should be in the search for one certain and self-evident proposition. Therefore, all contemporary advance in philosophy must begin by calling that starting point into question, thus calling metaphysics into basic question again too. Poor Descartes hoped that philosophy would never be in motion again after his time, but his suggestion of a single, certain starting point and a single, certain procedure simply raises all the basic questions again instead of settling them once and for all.

D. The Self as Source

Much contemporary philosophy seems to assume that the self is the obvious—or at least the only available—starting point for metaphysics, but this assumption itself raises a basic metaphysical question. "Soul" is an important concept to both Plato and Aristotle, and it is true that it was psychological investigation which led Plotinus to his discovery of the centrality of the principle of unity. Yet for none of these metaphysicians is the self by any means the only available starting point for metaphysics. Why should this idea have come to dominate Descartes and most of modern metaphysics? The answer to this question is again connected to the primacy which Descartes gives to the quest for certainty and to the necessity for immediacy. As should be obvious and as we have indicated in discussing Descartes, our aim has not been so much to outline the basic features of his thought as to raise the question of the assumptions upon which it proceeds. The problem of the self is a good example of a metaphysical question, and it is particularly appropriate with Descartes, since he criticized all thought before him for not achieving certainty and claimed to have discovered a new beginning which would allow it. We should now look at that beginning itself in a critical manner.

Concentration upon the self as the starting point and ground of all metaphysics is one way of restricting philosophy in order to assure its success; it is a narrowing of scope during a retreat in the face of an attack. If we cannot be certain in our theories about the basic categories of all things—as, for example, the One and the Many—then perhaps where the self is concerned we can be more certain and thus be able to complete philosophy's goal on that more immediate ground. In restricting the starting point of philosophy to the self, our interest in providing a ground for certainty in metaphysics and in developing a necessary doctrine is assumed. If we surrender such a view of the goal of metaphysics, the self becomes no more natural a starting point than any object, and the world as a whole actually does seem to be the natural direction for our attention. To make the self the exclusive datum and preoccupation for metaphysics is to make an assumption which involves its own assumptions, and these must be inspected closely. If the primary concern of metaphysics is not identified with an analysis of the self and its knowledge, metaphysics is free to become many other things—even a formulation of the principles of all Being.

Descartes, as well as others, felt that the self could be isolated and considered as something which did not involve either the body or other extended objects. Without examining Descartes's ulterior motives in desiring to isolate the self for such consideration, the question does arise as to whether this task of isolating the self can in fact be accomplished. More important questions are raised: What does this isolation assume about the nature of the self? Can we accept such assumptions? For Descartes, of course, the essence of the self is to be a "thinking thing." As natural as such a concentration on thought may seem to be for philosophy, there is a serious question as to whether such a view is acceptable, even if its assumption aided Descartes in finding (or supposing that he found) the self-evident and certain proposition which he sought. Aristotle, for one, denies that the soul can be defined except as the form of a natural body; and Plato, for all his stress on the separability and immortality of the soul, argued that the soul is composed of a mixture of reason with the passions and the will. The soul does much more than think, and an understanding of its thought may involve and demand a comprehensive grasp of these other aspects.

Clearly the problem involved in taking the self as a starting point is that the self is neither a neutral nor a commonly accepted concept; and it may be that the soul is indefinable except in the context of a larger theory, which is what Spinoza actually suggests. There has been a strong and almost unconscious desire in modern philosophy to find some neutral and indisputable starting point, some datum or data—that which is simply the given—which would be "phenomena" for the phenomenologists or "sense data" for recent empiricists. While it might be easier if some such given ground, untouched by theory, were available, the advocates of any school which stresses such an indisputable base have failed to agree with one another. This would seem to indicate that philosophy does not have open to it as an alternative the use of a first principle which itself cannot be questioned.

Even if the self, or Descartes's *Cogito ergo sum*, or phenomena, or common sense, or language were in themselves solid starting points beyond all doubt or challenge, the question always remains as to whether one ought to accept such a point as the philosophical beginning place. Thus metaphysics is continually called back into play as the criticism of alternative first principles, since no one such principle can establish itself forever to the exclusion of all others, even if certain advocates agree among themselves to assume for a time some one starting point without question.

E. The Isolation of Thought

Perhaps the self will turn out to be neither a neutral beginning point nor an obvious one, but will be discovered instead to be an entity the nature of which can be made clear only in the context of a more elaborate set of principles (empirical psychology notwithstanding). If so, we are forced to question our ability to isolate thought, and to fix philosophical concern exclusively on thought and its processes rather than on the structure of things. Metaphysics has sometimes been considered to be a "product of pure thought," but this view depends entirely on an agreement to isolate thought from things. To be sure, Kant breaks the connection and analyzes "pure reason," but this separation of thought from things is perhaps the main assumption of Kant's view that calls for serious examination.

Aristotle and Plato both held that thought takes its structure from the objects which it apprehends. On the other hand, Kant contended that we cannot know things as they are, and Descartes separated thought and the self from physical nature. It appears evident, then, that the question of the isolation of thought from things is a fundamental assumption which must first be questioned; otherwise, the basis of our metaphysics will simply be determined for us by default.

There is a certain attractiveness to "realism" as a theory of knowledge—that is, to the theory that the mind conforms to and grasps objects just as they exist. But it is important to note that Descartes and other modern philosophers reacted against such a theory of knowledge primarily because they demanded certainty. If the mind has the structure of all things for its object, and if thought can take on as many forms as there are forms of Being, then the entire enterprise does have a certain directness about it. But this suggestion also opens up the scope of philosophy so widely that it seems difficult, if not impossible, to achieve certainty. The attempt either to isolate thought or to use the self as a starting point is primarily a result of the demand for certainty in theory, and our questioning should begin precisely at this point.

It is by now notorious that those who begin with the self, or with thought in isolation, often never manage to establish any accepted way to extend philosophy beyond that basis. In this case, any certainty which they achieve is of a very restricted kind, or else the legitimacy of their attempts to extend further a knowledge derived from the self and thought is highly disputed. Descartes begins by finding that he can doubt every proposition except the one asserting his own existence. He is very dubious of extending this basis for certainty to any direct knowledge of the physical world, but he does think that the certainty of thought leads him necessarily to the existence of God. Thus, he offers his version of Anselm's famous "ontological argument" for God's existence, but Descartes's version is significantly different. Any approach to God seems to indicate a great deal about one's metaphysical assumptions, even if it tells us very little more about God. (For example, the primary queston at issue in Hume's *Dialogues on Natural Religion* is not his view of God, but the basis which he gives to all philosophical reasoning—that is, a reference to immediate impressions.)

Those who have examined Descartes's route—from a certain knowledge of self-existence on to a certainty about God—never really do seem to find a clear certainty involved in the inference. And

God is important to Descartes, for once God is introduced, he provides the basis for all philosophical certainty. God does this by guaranteeing thought and by removing radical skepticism concerning knowledge derived from the senses. Descartes simply outlines quickly what God's nature is as Descartes sees it. The philosopher's haste indicates his own lack of metaphysical sensitivity where uncertainties about God are concerned, however subtle he may be where self-knowledge is the issue.

Perhaps, even more than he uses the self, Descartes uses God to provide philosophy with a neutral starting point, and therefore, he does not question how to describe him. Because we cannot begin with any single object, God's nature becomes clear, not at the beginning of an inquiry, but only as the result of a metaphysical analysis of a number of principles. This fact we learn clearly from the contrast between the Gods of Plato, Aristotle, and Plotinus—their view of God is drawn, not from the observation of an object in the world, but from the general theory which each develops. Certainty may be a questionable philosophical goal, but to assume either the self or thought about God as a neutral starting point is possible only by the use of a number of first principles, each of which must first be defended and not simply assumed.

VII

SPINOZA
AND SUBSTANCE

If the modern age was to be able to provide necessity and certainty for its metaphysics, it had to establish criteria—or, preferably,
one criterion—by which certainty could be determined. Descartes
felt that by using a method of systematic doubt he could come to at
least one indubitable true proposition—the assertions of the self's
existence—and that this would then lead on to other equally certain
propositions (for example, the assertion of God's existence). He
hoped that then any prospective indubitable proposition could be
tested by at least one certainly true proposition—the assertion of the
self's existence—and that this would then lead on to other equally
certain propositions—for example, the assertion of God's existence.
He hoped that then any prospective indubitable proposition could
be tested by comparison with certain key features of the first basic
proposition. In order to test propositions against an indubitable
base, Descartes proposed a criterion of "clarity and distinctness";
that is, only ideas so clear and distinct that no one could doubt them
would be granted certainty.

However, when such criteria are established, two sorts of problems spring up: (1) the difficulties involved in pinning down precisely the meaning of the criteria—for example, what constitutes

clarity and distinctness—and (2) the refusal by some to accept these criteria—a refusal which usually takes the form of proposing alternate criteria. Since Descartes's time, such problems have beset all moderns who have wanted to establish philosophy securely on a single base, and this includes even those who have formulated criteria that exclude metaphysical theory from being a part of philosophy.

A. The Criteria for Certainty

Hume proposed *immediate impressions* as ultimate data for philosophical construction and *custom* as the ultimate philosophical criterion. Some do not accept these standards, and no obvious fact about the world forces anyone to do so when other standards are also available. The modern dream of uniting all men on a single philosophical basis seems to be doomed, both by the sheer impossibility of finding a single agreed-upon basis which is not itself subject to further dispute, and by the existence of multiple standards as possible alternatives. It would seem as if our world has both too loose and too complex a structure to satisfy this demand for singularity and certainty of theory.

God seems to be the original rebel against the modern cause, since he refused to create a rigid world on the basis of a single theoretical structure which could then be used to interpret it. Yet even if some do agree to accept, say, Hume's "impressions" as providing an ultimate philosophical touchstone, the history of modern empiricism indicates that these apparently simple criteria are not at all so simple in their application. Exactly what Descartes means by "clear and distinct," although this phrase appears on the surface to be simple, in practice actually becomes as complex as Hume's "impressions." When this happens, the simplicity of the criteria is lost, and to keep insisting upon the criteria merely starts an argument rather than ends all disagreement.

As we will see with Spinoza, modern philosophers all assume that there is a close, if not rigid parallel between metaphysical theory and the structure of Being itself. In criticizing this assumption, some critics have thought that all of philosophy, both past and present, has been based on this theory. But in fact this parallel seems to be a more modern assumption—one tied to the modern philosophers' obsession with achieving certainty. No evidence can be found prior to

Descartes's time to show that any philosopher thought his theory would either close off all further theory or serve as a basis upon which all future metaphysical construction would proceed.

Perhaps the major problem of metaphysics, then, is to determine the status which its written theories have, and then to come to terms with the existence of a multiplicity of theoretical structures in a discipline that seeks to describe Being itself. Making such decisions need not call for the development of a theory of the evolution of theory. One way to answer the problem of the multiplicity of theoretical structures is to treat theory as if it fits some evolving historical pattern. Yet this suggestion itself is only one theory about the plurality of theories, and it must not be assumed uncritically to be true.

In trying to understand modern philosophy, it is important to grasp the implications of this desire to establish a metaphysics which is capable of closing off permanently all further fundamental debate on the first principles of things. But it is equally important not to assume this goal without appraising it critically as one of the first issues which anyone must face in tackling the problems of metaphysics. Do we seek one final and true theoretical scheme? If so, how can this goal be defended? And, if not, how can the goal and the status of theory be presented? It is interesting, and perhaps ironic, that the Roman Catholic Church, which was so quick to see the theological dangers in much of modern philosophy, itself fell victim to the most fundamental and questionable of modern assumptions—that of the possibility for and the desirability of absolute certainty and finality in theoretical matters. (The present internal warfare going on in the Church largely centers around an attack of this long-held assumption.) Neither classical philosophy nor the New Testament seems in any way overly concerned about the possibility for absolute certainty, but modern metaphysics definitely has been.

B. What Constitutes Self-Sufficiency?

Just as Aristotle began by discussing Plato's philosophy, and Plotinus began by commenting on Plato's *Dialogues*, and just as each one developed some quite unique and independent theories from this process, so Spinoza first wrote on Descartes's philosophy. This fact leads us to ask what it is that one can learn by commenting on the thought of another man. We ought to suspect that metaphysics cannot be done in isolation, but that it needs the material support of previous theory as perhaps its most important orienting point. In any case, Descartes proposed a criterion of clarity and distinctness, and this seems to have led Spinoza to ask the basic question as to just how independent and distinct the objects and events in the world really are. Hume's definition of "impressions" assumes the absolute distinctness in existence of each individual thing, and Descartes's "clarity" certainly would appear to depend upon our ability to isolate one item so that it may be brought into sharp focus and be uncomplicated by entangling relations. In order to achieve ultimacy, such criteria as Hume and Descartes propose seem to depend upon a correspondence between the world's structure and their own assumptions. This parallel is, of course, the most important question.

Spinoza goes on to elaborate a theory about the structure of Being—a theory which is very far from allowing any individual entity to be distinct in itself. In fact, Spinoza's *Ethics* asserts almost the opposite—namely, that no item in the world can ultimately be isolated for understanding. Rather, because of the subtle and complex interrelatedness of all things, any independent phenomenon can finally be understood only by tracing out its place in the structure of things as a whole. Although such a theory does rule out the simplicity and easy finality of either Hume's proposal of a test by individual and distinct impressions, or Descartes's more theoretical criteria of clarity and distinctness, for Spinoza it does not at all rule out conclusive knowledge. He remains a modern in his love of simplicity and what he took to be the finality of mathematics. This theory does mean, however, that knowledge is transformed quite radically in its conception, and that the task of achieving it is made much more complex than was imagined earlier.

Spinoza goes about questioning how clarity and distinctness are achieved largely by asking what constitutes "self-sufficiency." From Aristotle's time on, self-sufficiency has been the property by reference to which meaning is given to the term "substance." That is, substance is that which is self-sufficient and therefore capable of existing alone. A man can exist alone, and so he has substantial existence, but his smiles cannot exist without him—hence, smiles are not substantial. Medieval theologians had stressed emphatically the dependence of all nature on God. Spinoza was excommunicated as a nonorthodox Jew and certainly he was not a Christian in theory. But he does stand as a primary example of an independent philosophical theologian who is basically a metaphysician and yet is much influenced by theological theory and questions.

Spinoza became convinced that if the definition of "substance" were taken strictly, then only one being met the qualification of absolute self-sufficiency—namely, God himself. This in itself might not have been too radical a conclusion, but Spinoza went on to link it with the traditional assertion of the dependence of all of creation on God, and he considered the two concepts necessarily connected. Thus, *Substance* becomes Spinoza's name for God. But this name means not God taken in dependence, but God only when he is taken together with the whole of nature.

Aristotle asserted that we understand a thing when we know its causes. Since knowledge concerns really only a small portion of the world, excluding the whole realm of the accidental and of practical affairs, to achieve this causal understanding is not too difficult. Now Spinoza expands this notion of causal understanding and treats it more strictly. Aristotle's Unmoved Mover was not the cause of all things, and so the Unmoved Mover's thought was concerned only with himself and with a hard core of essential and limited causes. Spinoza's *Substance*, on the other hand, is an omnipotent Creator-God, and because of this nothing can now be dismissed as accidental. God's vision may focus specifically on certain areas (on what Spinoza calls the *attributes* as distinguished from the *modes*), but all the world's events become *essential* in the last analysis. Thus, nothing can be left outside the scope of understanding, which is something that Aristotle did in order to achieve his goal of completed knowledge. For Spinoza, objects of knowledge are taken to be infinite in number, and the understanding of any one depends on tracing out the causal relationships which exist among them all, including every aspect of God.

One interesting consequence of taking this ultimate interconnection of all causal relationships so strictly is that God and man become mutually interdependent. It is not that God and man are equal, but God's self-sufficiency cannot be defined independently either of man or of the created order. God would not be God unless he created as he did, and this involves viewing man as being necessary to God's being. In fact, man is a part of Substance. This term now takes in together what formerly had been distinguished as God and Nature.

To understand God one must come to see his connection to man and to all of nature, and how all the parts stand in causal relationship to one another. To understand man one needs to rise to the infinite intellect of God, an accomplishment which Spinoza sees as perfectly possible if the human intellect is properly improved. The finite intellect must come to view man's own place in the connected order of all things, just as God, in his eternal act of creating all things, sees man's place as part of actualizing the whole of his nature.

A certain aspect of ultimate duality remains even in this interconnected whole. For viewed under the aspect of eternity, which is God's mode of understanding, time is not present. Time is real for man, and it constitutes his ordinary mode of apprehension. However, insofar as man seeks full knowledge of nature, he rises toward and is at least momentarily identical with God's way of viewing all things eternally. According to Spinoza's theory, man does not have too far to go in order to do this, since no gulf separates him from God. He is part of God's nature, not in that he himself is infinite, but only insofar as the two are taken together and understood as one Substance. Substance, moreover, is capable of independent existence only if it is a whole made up of every part of Being. The job of the human intellect is to "become God." It cannot cease to be finite, but it can widen its causal perspective to understand all things in their natural interdependence. If this is achieved—and it is at least theoretically possible—then Descartes's desired certainty will be the result.

C. Absolute Infinity

In attempting to understand Substance, Spinoza follows the model of mathematical axioms and deductive propositions. Below Substance he divides all things into *attributes* and *modes*. Two examples of attributes are thought and extension, but the fact is that, like Plotinus, Spinoza desires that as much as possible should be actual, and so he asserts that the attributes are infinite in number. Since we ordinarily know all things either as one form of thought or extension (as idea or as matter), it follows that we in fact are immediately aware of only two from among an actual infinity of attributes. However, this does not seriously damage our possibility to obtain complete knowledge, since Spinoza postulates that the attributes are all "parallel." This means that they do not proceed in causal independence from one another, but that each actually reflects the same essential structure. Because of this, to know one attribute is essentially to know the structure of them all, so that the absence of direct knowledge of all of the infinite attributes is not an essential limitation on knowledge.

Attributes are forms in which our intellect apprehends Substance, and modes are the particular forms which an attribute takes. For instance, physical bodies are modes of extension and represent the way in which the intellect understands that attribute. Thus, we may go about gathering additional knowledge of a variety of modes, or we can equally as well understand all things by following out the particular expressions of any one attribute. Since all attributes are joined in a causal network, to begin at any one spot is essentially an attempt to see the whole structure. In this sense there are no blind alleys for the intellect. Since nothing can exist in isolation, nothing can lead the intellect astray. In our understanding we do, however, seek increased scope. Therefore, the failure of understanding could not lie in selecting either trivial or irrelevant material. In their origin, the social sciences seem to share Spinoza's metaphysics at this point. Our only danger lies in failing to expand the intellect's scope constantly.

It follows that Substance is not simply infinite, which alone would be sufficient to foil Aristotle's understanding. Substance is, in fact, *absolutely infinite*. It is easy enough to see that this must be so from considering attributes and modes. Each attribute is itself infinite, since Being would be restricted if it were not carried out to its ultimate possible limit. The number of attributes is also infinite, since it would be equally restrictive—and thus undesirable in Spinoza's terms—to stop with only two attributes, namely, thought and extension. Within the attributes, there are both finite and infinite modes. In addition to simple infinity—one kind of thing carried without limits to its infinite extent—there must now also be an absolute infinity—an infinity of kinds, each infinite in itself.

Aristotle would be horrified at the suggestion of absolute infinity, but Spinoza is not afraid of infinity. Rather than excluding it for the sake of reason, he makes the grasp of an absolute infinity reason's ultimate and possible goal. Such a "reason" is, of course, not the limited reason of man considered as an independent substance in himself. That is a status which Aristotle gave to man. For Spinoza, intellect must now be seen as a part of God's self-understanding, and thus it becomes capable of achieving the same divine perspective.

Clarity is Spinoza's goal, just as it was Descartes's. Philosophers of the early modern period seemed to think that philosophy's failure to unite upon one metaphysical theory is the result of a failure to test and to specify the limits and abilities of our intellect. Locke and Hume, as well as Descartes and Spinoza, sought a way to ground philosophy in greater unity by attending first to the intellect's nature, and then by finding some sure test for the validity of its operation. Unfortunately for the success of this interesting attempt, each philosopher had his own theory of the intellect's scope and a criterion by which the success of the theory could be securely judged.

At this point, the differences between theories are not minor but major, and this can be seen by comparing how divergent Descartes's and Spinoza's proposals are for the achievement of clarity. One man seeks clarity and certainty by concentrating on a single self-evident proposition as a touchstone for all knowledge, while the other achieves his goal only by comprehending simultaneously the absolutely infinite extent of all of Substance, of God and man, and more of nature than sight can ever see.

D. Freedom and Emotion

Spinoza's major metaphysical treatise is entitled *Ethics*, and this title indicates that his metaphysical proposals cannot be understood without his ethical intent. On the other hand, Descartes could never develop a full moral theory that was clearly related to his beginning point, and Aristotle made ethics into a practical affair not subject to the same rigor as metaphysical inquiry. Spinoza's *Ethics* tolerates no such separation of speculation and human practice. The reason for metaphysical construction, it is clear from the very beginning, is simply to provide the framework necessary for moral achievement. To understand how this can be done, we must first understand what Spinoza means by "freedom." What the term does *not* mean, first of all, is the possibility of adopting a variety of alternatives or the possibility of things being different from what in fact they are. To wish nature to be different is to ask for God to be different from what he is, since nature as we know it is simply an extension of God's substance.

Freedom means a lack of outside interference in the development and action of a thing. In the natural development of the powers of the thing, freedom means that it encounters no block to its expression. In this sense, God is the only free being. Since there is only one Substance, nothing outside his nature exists to limit or to impede him. Man, on the other hand, can never achieve full freedom, since his existence as a finite thing means that his natural drive to achieve a full expression for his powers is always subject to a threat from outside himself.

Still, freedom for man is possible in the intellectual sense because no fact can be other than it is. To come to understand this is, in a certain way, to share in God's freedom by an intellectual grasp of the causes which establish things as they are. The result of this understanding is the dissipation of useless and frustrating emotions, since these arise only through ignorance of the causes which establish all things. A fruitless attempt to change a fixed order, or the mental anguish of protesting against it, provokes passion, but a proper understanding can eliminate this danger. Man becomes free to the extent that he achieves God's self-understanding and thus shares God's freedom from useless passion.

This freedom involves the fact that "good" means simply existence, so that all things are good to the extent that they exercise their full powers to exist. Nothing can prevent this development except a failure to grasp the causes which determine all things. Rightly to understand your nature, its causes and its powers, and the necessary connection of these to Substance as a whole is to understand that "good" means fulfillment and that "evil" means the failure to achieve what Spinoza calls an "adequate idea" of things. Thus, the ethical life is intimately bound up with the intellectual life and its successful achievement, and is not simply a matter of practical action in the way that Aristotle had thought of ethics. The "intellectual love of God" is the goal of all men, according to Spinoza, and it is the one goal which can be shared in by all without exclusion. To "love" God in this way means to seek an adequate understanding. This is how God understands himself—by grasping all of Substance under the aspect of eternity.

To be diminished in our potential power is to "suffer" and to undergo a "passive" emotion. This tendency toward passion is a path which men, as limited modes, cannot avoid, since their power inevitably conflicts with the development of the power of others. But emotion can be "active," too, in that man can understand the causes that determine things as they are and can connect them to the divine nature. When he achieves this understanding he does not suffer, but experiences joy. To achieve a greater degree of understanding is to pass into a higher existence. This potential is open to man, and it means to experience "joy" rather than "sorrow," since the latter is the result of a limiting emotion which is only confusedly understood. Just because man is a part of Substance and is never Substance itself, understanding the causes of emotion is a process which can never be completed. Progress can be made toward this goal, and this is done by improving the understanding through a knowledge of the necessity of causes, which thereby relieves the individual of inhibiting emotions which he need not bear. Metaphysical understanding is a means to ethical liberation.

E. The Divine Necessity

Problems arise for Spinoza's metaphysics over the goal which he outlines for it and from the scheme which he suggests for the achievement of that goal. Although he sought for certainty in theory and rejected contingency as not ultimate, there is little to suggest that Spinoza thought of his own theory as either the last metaphysics or as a conclusion without alternative. Perhaps the crux of our attention should center on the picture of the divine nature which he draws, since in his theory it is perfectly clear that this is the center of all philosophical understanding and ethical improvement. Why does Spinoza bind God to necessity without a choice? Because it is clear that man cannot have a freedom of alternatives unless God also has a contingency of choice. Why not, then, allow both God and Man more flexibility and alternatives in their choices? In order to answer this we must return to understand the cherished modern goal of necessity and certainty in metaphysics, and to the accompanying desire to complete the task of philosophy once and for all.

Clearly contingency in either God or man will involve a certain flexibility in theory too, since only an absolutely necessary world could be embodied in one theoretical framework perfectly so as to exclude all others. Man's freedom to be other than he is and God's choice to create in other forms than exist—both must be denied in the interest of reaching intellectual stability. Unless God is free, there can be no freedom in any secondary or lesser creatures, if we take "freedom" to mean an ability to be or to act so that things might be other than they are. Thus, in order to achieve the goal of certainty, necessity, and completion in metaphysical theory, God must be denied alternatives, and "will" must be eliminated as anything other than the desire for a true—that is, necessary—idea. Modern man has shown a tendency either to reject God or to bind him to necesssity in existence and action. If men tend toward the former, they do so on the ground that God inhibits man's freedom; he chooses the latter on the ground that an absolutely free God interferes with the intellectual goal of achieving an unalterable theoretical understanding. What metaphysics does to God is a good indication of both its intentions and its goals.

We understand the problems of a particular metaphysics, then, by some grasp of the role which is assigned to theory, and from the results which are expected from it. Were only one metaphysical position concerning freedom possible, for example, this would not be so. But since we grant that there are a variety of ways to interpret freedom, all the way from absolute contingency to strict necessity, it seems possible to see the reason for selecting one route over another only by grasping what a proposed theory intends to accomplish for itself. Since we are not at all agreed as to what philosophy is and as to what it can accomplish, when the assumptions of a given view become clear, the problems which that theory faces also become clear. The problems are then either capable of solution in that context, or insoluble, given the starting point. The problem of basic assumption is the primary "metaphysical problem" upon which individual problems depend for their explicit definition. Individual problems—the problems of freedom, time, Substance, order, and so forth—do not exist independently of any individual theory but take their particular shape and definition only as the meaning assigned to philosophical theory is made clear.

Furthermore, it is impossible to treat any problem simply in the abstract. In that sense, there is no "problem of freedom" simply in itself, but there are only men who act and who work out their decisions. Freedom becomes a "problem" only as a basic metaphysics is developed. For instance, with Spinoza we come to see the implication of freedom, and we find a way to develop that concept within a theoretical context only as his theory is elaborated. It follows that, if we are not to be the victims of the confines of one theoretical structure, we need to understand how each framework determines the formulation of the problem and sets the limits within which its solution is possible.

Freedom becomes a "problem" for Spinoza as he develops the ethical goal of philosophy and as he works out the nature of his

God. Clearly no solution to the question of freedom is possible without a challenge to these basic assumptions—that is, without a solution which is not restricted in its extent by Spinoza's original definitions. In this sense Kant develops a doctrine of freedom which is just as indicative of his metaphysics as Spinoza's definition of freedom is of his. "Problems" appear as a metaphysical theory is fleshed out, and they are "solved" as that basic context is challenged and thus altered. In this way new alternatives are opened up for theory.

VIII

KANT AND FREEDOM

In comparing Plato and Aristotle, we recognized the important distinction between a philosopher who expresses and develops his views in a technical terminology which is carefully defined (Aristotle) and another (Plato) who generally speaks in ordinary terms, although concepts do emerge as central and develop special meanings (for example, those of Form and Soul). In the work of Kant we find the epitome of the use of technical terminology. Almost anyone can discuss Platonic questions; Plato himself set them in the form of ordinary discussion, although distinctions and more careful definition do come out as an end product. With Kant, however, unless you come close to speaking and thinking as he does, you cannot understand or even discuss his metaphysics. Since we are interested in treating metaphysics critically, however, we must neither accept this terminology without question nor treat it as ultimate.

A. The Origins of Technical Terminology

We understand something more about Kant's view when we grasp why it seems both natural and obvious to him that we must proceed by the use of an elaborately defined terminology, one which itself develops a structure of relationships. For Kant is convinced that

91

although we are in some direct contact with the objects of the world, our minds do not have immediate contact with entities as they are in themselves. Kant's task is to specify in what way and through what mediation our contact with objects is made. The basic root of Kant's metaphysics—the assumption which seems so basic to him that he proceeds from it and never questions it—is that although we can know things, we cannot know them as they are in themselves, but only as they are affected by our ways of perceiving and understanding them. If, then, knowledge must be drawn from the mind's self-understanding, elaborately defined technical terms do seem necessary if we are ever to have a firm structure upon which the mind can rely.

Perhaps the simplest and yet most important technical distinction which Kant relies upon is that between the *a priori* and the *a posteriori*. Delete these terms from the Kantian vocabulary and all would be changed in an instant. *A priori* means prior to or before experience, but it is most important to understand that this priority is not simply temporal. An *a posteriori* knowledge, on the other hand, is that knowledge which comes from or is dependent upon experience. Of course, it is easy to see that everything depends on what is and is not taken to be found in "experience," and, in a way, much of Kant's analysis is an exploration of this question. No fixed meaning has to be ascribed to the term "experience" at the beginning of any philosophical inquiry, since what can and cannot be included in this term is not obvious. On the surface, nothing is excluded as possible within "experience" until the adoption of some philosophical view leads us to exclude or to include certain things. It is not only important, but actually necessary to avoid assuming any philosophical definition of the limits of experience until a careful consideration is made of the ways in which the term "experience" is to be applied.

Objects in the world are not *a priori*. They simply *are*. Such technical terminology does not spring from things; it concerns our experience of them. Technical terms are defined and set by us; they are neither given to us nor is their use externally commanded. Upon analysis, we may wish to adopt such technical terminology if it makes possible the best available philosophical approach, but we should not do this until after we have first considered seriously the question of the origin of a technical vocabulary. We must realize clearly what is determined for us by the assumptions contained within a terminology whenever we adopt one; and, most importantly, we need to know what alternatives we might have if we should find that view uncongenial. Things are not "impressions," but Hume suggests that we adopt this terminology to speak about them. Half the philosophical battle is won or lost, depending on your view, when the implications of any technical terminology are accepted—or rejected and reformulated.

In order to understand Kant, then, we must become skilled in the manipulation of an elaborate set of technical concepts and, next, develop subtlety in discerning the special relationships which hold between them. What is the origin of the definition of such terms for Kant, and what alternatives might there be to his theory of their ultimate origin? It seems clear that the answers to these questions may be found by reflecting on the title of Kant's major work, *The Critique of Pure Reason*. A "critique" is an inquiry into assumptions; it is an attempt to disclose what is prerequisite to that which we take as obvious.

Cut off from the ability to investigate Being itself in the way that Aristotle did with the concepts of matter and form, Kant decided that reason itself has a structure, although it is one which we do not see directly. Nevertheless, "critical" inquiry can bring reason's structure to light. From this inquiry into reason's necessary structure, then, technical terminology seems to rise naturally for Kant, and not as if he himself had invented the meanings to be given to these important terms. To those who follow Kant, it will also seem to be true that the technical structures named by his terminology arise not from objects themselves or from the world's basic structure, but from the very structure of reason itself in its philosophical employment. Perhaps the basic metaphysical question that is raised indirectly by Kant is the problem of identifying the source of the validity of the technical distinctions which actually shape Kant's thought. This problem must be carefully considered by anyone interested in metaphysics and sensitive to its problems.

As we shall see, and as philosophers have discovered for over a century, the assumption made here about the use and origin of philosophical terminology has widespread implications concerning the form which metaphysics can take and what it can hope to accomplish. Once inside the Kantian castle, there is little left to do but to explore the maze of its corridors. A metaphysician must first of all ask himself whether it is even necessary to enter this passageway, as Kant thought that it was. This question is particularly crucial now that we can see the results of Kant's explorations—both their range

and their limits. In metaphysics we are free, not to avoid all terminology or all limitations, but to choose new terms and to set new
limits freely.

B. The Assumptions of Experience

Because of what we have indicated, it seems that to play Kant's
game is an all-or-nothing affair, although many have found its intricacies both fascinating and rewarding. If technical terminology
shapes our thought in unavoidable ways when its definitions are
assumed, it also makes certain structures visible to the mind which
would be impossible to see unaided. Given Kant's special definition
of "experience," we see that his aim is one of learning about experience by indirect inference. That is, we want to get from "experience" (as defined), not what can be gained by direct inspection of its
specific content—for example, the image of a ship sailing down a
river—but some idea of the degree and manner in which the mind
affects the structure and, hence, the necessity of experience itself.
The discovery of the general structure of all experience whatsoever—
this is Kant's aim. Of course, the possibility of such a discovery
depends on the fact that certain basic limits have been set to "experience" in its technical definition, such that, according to this
meaning, neither God nor the Platonic Forms can be "experienced"
as Plato thought they could.

What concepts, in addition to the "given" of an experience, are
necessary for our understanding of experience—either this particular
experience or any possible experience? We have already seen the
importance of the special terms *a priori* and *a posteriori*, but two
more technical concepts matched with them are almost more crucial
in their assumptions—namely, *analytic* and *synthetic*. "Analytic"
refers to what is not new but is simply analyzed out of a given
concept, whereas the term "synthetic" calls attention to the actual
addition to knowledge of a factor not derivable from the concept
itself.

We might question whether, in fact, the world is put together on
the basis of this interesting technical relationship, but in any case it
is clear that Kant thinks our minds, at least, operate on this basis.
From this premise Kant moves on to discover that our understanding
has certain *forms* which are necessary to its structure and which are
unavoidable in its employment—namely, space and time—and that
reason cannot operate without functioning in terms of certain fixed

general *categories*. Neither of these structures provides us with any specific information, but our critique has revealed these structures to be assumed in every movement of the understanding.

It is almost impossible to deal with Kant either briefly or simply, due to some of the reasons indicated above. It is not our intent to try to do so here, or even to focus on some part of the crucial technical terminology already mentioned and to question its assumptions. Rather, since our primary interest lies in the problems of metaphysics and in seeing what happens to them on Kantian grounds, let us focus on one crucial issue: *freedom*. In considering Spinoza, we argued that the particular interpretation of "freedom" is indicative of the direction of any metaphysics. Thus, it might be possible to consider Kant in briefer perspective by focusing on the doctrine of freedom which results from his scheme, and then we can leave the reader to train himself further in the internal intricacies of the Kantian technical vocabulary. There are many ways to approach Kant. One approach would be to consider his definition of metaphysics and his antimetaphysical restrictions, plus the way in which he allows metaphysical problems to be dealt with. Yet for a brief treatment, his position on freedom is perhaps more revealing of his own metaphysical position—that is, of the consequences of his own basic assumptions.

Kant's metaphysical position involves primarily his divorce of the mind from all direct contact with things as they are, his pursuit of the necessary forms of the understanding which govern our grasp of all experience, and the structuring of his technical vocabulary, which for him is determined by the structure of reason itself. All of these are basic assumptions that require metaphysical challenge, but perhaps an inquiry into these first principles of Kantian thought can best be carried out by examining the results to which they lead Kant regarding freedom. No first principles are neutral, but, as befits first principles, they determine the ground upon which a question is to be considered, and perhaps set the limits on the interpretation which can be given. What was Kant "forced" to do in defining freedom, and what light does this shed for our project of testing his first principles against other alternatives?

C. Between Two Worlds

By employing the distinctions which he adopted, Kant develops a theory of two worlds—the *noumenal* and the *phenomenal*. The relationship between these two realms puzzled Kant—and everyone else ever since the appearance of his *Critique*. The *phenomenal* world (the world as experienced) is that which appears to us, and it is conditioned by the forms of intuition and the categories for our understanding of it. The *noumenal* world is the world and its objects as they exist independently of our mind's grasp and the structuring of them in knowledge. The noumenal world (the world in itself) may or may not be either close to or identical with our structured phenomenal world, but we can never step from behind the necessary phenomenal structuring to compare the two worlds in order to solve this problem. As selves, we too are both noumenal and phenomenal, so that the self participates in two worlds, just as all experienced things do.

The strictness of Kant's "deduction" of the structures that are necessary to our understanding—structures which thus are constitutive of the phenomenal world for us all—forbids the extension of what we find necessary for the understanding of our experience to apply beyond the limits of our experience—that is, beyond the phenomenal world—to the noumenal. This limitation has the advantage of allowing certain things to be possible in the noumenal realm which our discovery of the necessary structure of the phenomenal world would otherwise have ruled out. Such is the case with freedom. One of the categories of the understanding which is necessarily applicable to all experience (as Kant defines experience) is that of necessary causal connection. Therefore, all experience and every object in the phenomenal world is subject to this rigid causal determinism. This is convenient for the regularity of science, as Kant see it, but it also excludes freedom for the self-as-phenomenon. However, this exclusion of freedom in the face of necessary causality can be applied validly only to the phenomenal world, and this leaves the possibility of freedom as a characteristic of selves an open question in the noumenal realm. Because Kant feels that morality demands free action as a basis for moral responsibility, he goes on to postulate the existence of freedom as characteristic of noumenal selves, even though his critique has bound the phenomenal world to the necessary operation of the physical laws of causality.

In order to achieve freedom, Kant has had to split two worlds apart and refuse to let them be reduced to any one set of governing principles. This has perplexed Kant's followers, and it has also stood as an amazing achievement. This split comes as a consequence of the whole structure which he has adopted, and any questions concerning the resulting doctrine of freedom must be directed to those initial assumptions. Our first questions where freedom is concerned are whether the world is in fact best divided in this way, and whether it ought to be distinguished in terms of this developed technical vocabulary.

It is interesting to note that Kant, no less than Plato, has two distinct worlds. He has not escaped Plato's division, although he has drawn it in unique ways and has characterized it in quite different terms. We are left "between two worlds," and our only question now is whether Kant has correctly divided them or whether he has led us into distinctions which are not quite accurate and that need be neither accepted nor characterized by using his terms.

A new role for metaphysics certainly develops as a consequence of Kant's distinctions, and, interestingly enough, what metaphysics can do and what it is prevented from doing simply follow as a result of the basic set of distinctions which Kant offers. In this case, what metaphysics is becomes the result of prior considerations. Yet what is metaphysics in its classical meaning—as distinguished from the special meaning assigned to it by Kant as "transcending experience"—except an inquiry into basic assumptions? Our question is: What does metaphysics depend upon if it is not itself a fundamental inquiry into the assumptions of any philosophical procedure— including Kant's?

D. A Kingdom Divided   ⊙

"And if a kingdom be divided against itself, that kingdom cannot stand" (Mark 3:24). In spite of this saying, Kant has dominated much of our thinking about freedom for over a century. The basic question here is whether "half a freedom" is enough. If we accept Kant's basic distinctions, we are forbidden by their structure to merge the two worlds—the phenomenal and the noumenal. Hence what applied to one—for example, necessity—need not apply to the other. In some sense, Kant knows that we can think on both sides of these limitations. However, if we accept his requirement for the "critical" grounding of all knowledge—namely, the requirement that knowledge must be based in some assumption which is necessary to the very possibility of experience—then we can think about the problem of freedom in one realm while considering necessary causality in the other. Still, we have no basis either for providing a solution or for rejecting one side. Kant has, in that sense, insured against any rejection of freedom; the very grounds of knowledge make its denial impossible.

Should this position on freedom seem unsatisfactory, it is possible to try to find a ground upon which to mediate between the two realms or even perhaps to join them. In this attempt, the "self" is a natural starting point, since it is the agent of freedom in the noumenal realm. The self is the immediate object which obviously lives under both realms, and, in the order of phenomena, it is clearly the source of the law of necessary causality through the analysis of its own process of understanding. Yet Kant himself refuses to bring the self as an object in among our other objects of experience, since, were it to be so considered, the possibility for the self's noumenal freedom would be lost. The necessity which the self discovered as assumed in its empirical understanding cannot be extended beyond the limit which necessity imposes. Because Kant excludes the self from the objects of experience, in some ways the self stands, in Kant's terms, gloriously a member of two realms in that it achieves freedom despite causality. On the other hand, as far as the ground for knowledge goes, the self is unalterably divided against itself. Can a self live two such lives for very long?

At this point we need to ask why it was necessary for Kant to take such a risk. Why was it so crucial to preserve freedom that Kant was willing to divide the self against itself without hope of any resolution? Kant shared the modern metaphysical assumption of the need for theoretical necessity, and yet he agreed with the result of Hume's breakdown of experience into "impressions" and "ideas." Given these independently existing entities, which ultimately are distinct in their existence (this is a grave metaphysical assumption and a first principle for Hume's thought), no necessity could be found. Kant went further than Hume and denied our ability to reach any objects as they are in themselves, and this is Kant's grave metaphysical assumption. The only possible place left for the discovery of necessity was not in things or even in theory, but in the mind's own structure. However, Kant had set out to avoid the skeptical consequence of Hume's metaphysical view of the world as composed of separately existing and unconnected "impressions." Although Kant could avoid skepticism by going beyond the necessities which he found inherent in the mind's structure for the reception of experience, how does this procedure affect Kant's other original metaphysical goals?

Kant tells us clearly that he wants to establish a basis for "God, freedom and immortality," and in order to do this he sets out to locate a new ground for metaphysics. The ground which he discovers will give him the desired modern metaphysical base of necessity in theory. However, not only is it impossible to extend Kant's basis of knowledge once it is discovered, but the very conditions for its discovery prevent its extension beyond the ground of experience, and this, at least by Kant's definition, excludes God. Furthermore, any extension of the principles of knowledge would actually have the effect of denying freedom, but providing a basis for freedom is certainly one of Kant's principal goals. Therefore, the extension of the new basis of knowledge must be doubly prohibited as being both invalid and undesirable in its consequences. It is to preserve Kant's original goals that this divided kingdom is made ultimate. But, we must ask, is no other avenue to these goals possible, and are no other philosophical premises available to us? Or must freedom be sacrificed for the goals of theoretical understanding?

E. Beyond or Behind Kant?

The basic metaphysical problem which Kant raises is: Which way are we to turn? At least according to one definition, Kant has now rendered metaphysics impossible, although in another way he has opened up the possibility of reaching metaphysical conclusions. The only problem is that this new way to approach metaphysics rests on a different basis from that of earlier thinkers, and it results in a split world. In some basic sense, Kant, in establishing his analysis of the principles necessarily assumed in all experience, has given us a new kind of metaphysics based on his critical method—namely, a metaphysics of experience. Admittedly, this is more limited in scope than is true of other masterpieces within the metaphysical tradition, but Kant's work does seek to uncover the set of first principles affecting all *experience*, even if our discovery of the basic structures of Being itself is rendered impossible by this very method. Some have been content to accept this limited meaning to metaphysics, but others have moved on to concentrate on one obvious link—the self—which Kant had said could not be known directly.

Obviously, if this crucial limitation can be overcome and a genuine basis uncovered for a direct knowledge of the self, then the crucial member of both of Kant's realms might also become the mediator between them. In a knowledge of the self's structure, it would seem, lies the key to uniting the divided kingdoms. Because of the supposed preferability of the self as an object which is invulnerable to doubt, we saw Descartes concentrate upon the self and its thought. Kant prohibited all such direct self-knowledge because he thought it impossible to achieve, but the problems raised by Kant's solutions simply redoubled the modern interest in making the self a primary center upon which metaphysics might be based. The stress on the primacy of the self as pure thought is developed by Descartes, and this stress arises again as a result of the tensions established by Kant's "separate but equal" kingdoms.

When we move on to consider Hegel we will see at least one way in which a discovery of the self puts metaphysics on a new basis. Yet, as far as the fundamental assumptions of Kant's thought are concerned, the primary metaphysical question is one of direction: Must we go behind or beyond Kant? Most philosophers have tried to go beyond; the phenomenologists, for example, have attempted to do so by making the self *directly* available, at least phenomenologically. Perhaps, however, for an understanding of metaphysics it is almost more important to ask: What assumptions lying behind Kant's metaphysics ought to be questioned? The philosophers who go "beyond Kant" do not do so, interestingly enough, by seriously challenging the basic proposition which he set down for philosophy—namely, that there is no direct access to the structure of things *in themselves* (but only *as experienced*). Kant's critics instead try to find ways to solve the basic paradoxes which result—for example, the paradox that the self is both bound and free. The attempt is made either by the introduction of new material or by questioning the detail of certain Kantian arguments—for example, the possibility of *a priori* synthetic knowledge.

Metaphysics should not assume the fundamental principles of any philosophical approach, but it should try to determine what these principles are and then consider them in the light of possible alternatives. Here a certain historical knowledge of other theories is indispensable to an understanding of metaphysical problems, since understanding metaphysics critically involves both the awareness of the existence of different basic assumptions for philosophical procedure, and some ability to compare and to evaluate the various sets of first principles. You cannot, then, be a metaphysician and be familiar with only one context and vocabulary for philosophy, however technically proficient you may become within these accepted limits. As a metaphysician, Kant himself set out the basic assumptions for his own inquiry, so that the way "behind Kant" is to bring to light his fundamental principles—those which form the basis for his procedure but are not themselves defended. We call these procedures into question; we ask in what sense philosophy has open to it different structuring points, and whether we might have available technical vocabulary and distinctions different from those which Kant pursued so ruthlessly to their ultimate conclusion.

IX

HEGEL AND REASON

In order to understand Kant we needed to master the complexities of a technical vocabulary. Where Hegel is concerned we have to learn the structure of a whole new world. Our ordinary thought processes are not at all sufficient for the understanding of Hegel's doctrine, although they may lead to their own correction and to a complete way of knowing—that is, when our own thought breaks down under the impact of Hegel's tortuous logic.

The "Hegelian" distinction so often made between "appearance" and "reality" actually belongs more to the British philosopher Francis Herbert Bradley, who translated Hegel's complexities into the King's English. Yet accepting this distinction will be helpful in our introduction to Hegel, since the source of the distinction does lie in Hegel's metaphysics. If we talk about "appearance" versus "reality," what have we already assumed about our understanding of the world?

The same distinction has often been applied to Plato, but although there is a similarity, the idea is basically misunderstood when it is attributed to the Platonic view. Plato did indeed think that knowledge from our senses could be misleading and, more important, that empirical data are not sufficiently stable to serve as a basis for knowledge. For Plato it was a vision of the Forms which illuminated the intelligible aspects in the real objects of the world. However, this vision does not transform them, nor does it turn our central attention away from the basic reality of the physical world which is simply before us.

With Hegel it is otherwise: When taken on their own, both the deliverances of our five senses and all immediate factual knowledge are incomplete (a charge which Plato never made). More than that, such information is misleading if it is simply taken as it comes to us. The development of true knowledge will reveal simple facts to be merely appearances of something more ultimate—namely, a process—and any individual fact or occurrence will seem partial and insubstantial until it is fitted into the whole pattern (an idea which is faintly reminiscent of Spinoza). How are we to discover this reality, and how will an understanding of it be obtained? And, when such an understanding is reached, how will this transform our understanding of what before seemed to be simple and evident facts, so that now the whole world is changed as a result of such metaphysical vision? Here is the source of the split in metaphysics since the nineteenth century—between those who seek the completion of this transformation and those who resist any such transformation and try to pry knowledge loose from the simple facts before them when taken just as they are.

"Realism" as a theory of knowledge (the view that our minds directly grasp the forms of independently existing objects by which the mind is affected and from which it draws its knowledge), and "common sense" theories, whether based upon a study of language or of sense data, are both to be understood as metaphysical reactions against the all-transforming effects of the Hegelian doctrine. Were it not for Hegel, must of the recent antimetaphysical polemic—the assertion of alternative first principles for philosophical investigation—would not make sense.

It is clear that Hegel genuinely thought something to be unreal about the world of simple fact which we find before us—a belief which no other metaphysician has had. That is, he thought that the world is misleading until it is transformed by the crucial effect of philosophical reason without which nothing can be grasped as real. Metaphysics, in this view, has more than a limited area for its operation; without its important transforming powers, nothing in the world can be understood. With Hegel, philosophy reached the utmost in the extravagance of its claim to centrality in all life, and the reactions to this claim have been so violent that many have either rejected or severely limited all philosophy as a constructive enterprise.

Yet we cannot react against Hegel's claims as being exaggerated without carefully considering the possibility of the truth of his basic principles. For if there is a reality to be discovered by reason—one which is present latently, but which is neither fully grasped nor developed in common experience—then to leave this task unexplored is to mistake what is before us as absolute when it is not so. Hegel poses for us most clearly the issue of what we can or cannot accept as "absolute."

Many other suggestions about the ultimate have been made, but since none has met with universal acceptance—neither the appeal to Hume's "impressions" nor the reference by Wittgenstein to "language games"—the question as to what forms philosophy's ultimate base is still open, and the issue continues to be alive. There is a certain simple appeal in accepting as ultimate something immediately before us, but that which common sense suggests must come up against Hegel's challenge that something more than common sense is needed to provide a basis for understanding a very complex world. Hegel argues that ultimacy lies only at the end of a long rational process, not at its beginning. He also suggests that the world we reach there may be quite different from the one we started with.

A. Spirit and Dialectic

In order to explore Hegel's proposal, it is important to grasp the force which animates it. The logic of understanding is a living process for Hegel, and its underlying forces must not be killed or frozen for simplicity's sake. Instead, they must be grasped as they are—in a complex of motion and development. In this case, *Spirit* becomes a central concept. Like Plato, Hegel does not consider motion to be irrational or unintelligible. Rather, he considers motion to be the very source of reason, and he regards reaching a decision on this question to be one of the major challenges to metaphysics. To grasp the action and the movement of Spirit—its phenomenology—is to fathom the inner working of reality. If Hegel is right, then not to follow this path is to be forever doomed to an apparently simple stability, something that is perhaps obvious on the surface but which nevertheless is not the source of reality. Understanding Spirit, of course, is closely bound up with a knowledge of the self, except that now the concept of Spirit becomes a larger concept than that of self, and it is only partially exemplified in individual selves.

In a sense, Hegel's *Phenomenology of Mind* can be regarded as an answer to the Kantian need for a direct grasp of the self; this is a knowledge which was unobtainable on Kant's terms due to the basic assumptions with which he began. However, for Hegel the self never really becomes empirically known, although consideration of the phenomenal self may be our starting point. The self is revealed only theoretically as its various pursuits unfold its structure and present it to us finally as theoretically transformed.

"Thinking" is central for Descartes, and Hegel does not disagree with the analysis of thinking as a starting point for philosophy. The problem of thought is another major issue that requires decision before other metaphysical problems can be attacked. Yet Hegel's "Spirit" is more comprehensive than Descartes's "thought," or at least its mode of procedure is vastly more complex. Descartes was mistaken only in his understanding of how far one had to go before anything could be "clear," and then, due to the complexity of their relations, the matters considered could never really be as "distinct" as he hoped that they would be.

As far as Hegel's methodology goes, perhaps the most important thing to understand is *dialectic*—how it proceeds and how it develops. If there is not a single firm structure which has always formed Being—if, instead, there has been a process of development—then a true understanding must start with the attempt to grasp the form of this process. Were this form arbitrary or contingent or subject to accidents, then the task would be very difficult. But Hegel was convinced that the development of all things falls within the embrace of one inevitable process. This makes *process* an ultimate category in terms of which all things are to be understood.

However, if all development is one process, rational and interconnected, then it may be grasped as such, and the problem of form need not defeat philosophy as Aristotle might have thought it would. Instead, process fulfills and embodies form in a rational manner. If we accept such an interconnected process as ultimate, then it is easy to see why things cannot be accepted as being either as simple or as obvious as they appear to be. They are not "just what they are and not another thing," but rather they are the result of many connections of causes in a process of development and are truly understood only in this manner. To seek greater simplicity is to deceive oneself and to dodge philosophy's enormous task.

A consideration of the meaning of "dialectic"—a term which is used in a simple form by Plato—indicates the complexity of process. No process is smooth, for every process is full of contradictions, oppositions, and even destruction. Only by understanding the negative and oppositional forces which have to be overcome in the process can we really ever reach an understanding of it. Even a simple logical conclusion is usually not uncovered except by a consideration of negative propositions; this is a fact which modern logic has learned. Logic, then, takes on a special meaning for Hegel, and it is never merely either the analysis of grammatical structure or the development of mathematical principles. We must always raise the question of logic and its relationship to metaphysics, and Hegel gives us his answer here: Logic is the grasp of the bare structure of the development of all things. Logic provides simply a beginning point for much that needs to be made concrete, but still it yields a bare skeleton which can be discerned in the process of the development of all things.

B. History and Reason

Aristotle discounted history as an unsuitable object of knowledge because it contained too much of the accidental. As a temporal process it was not rational in itself, but it became so only by reference to what was not itself in motion—the Unmoved Mover. Although Plato was more lenient about the possible rationality of some (but not all) motion, it was not until Hegel's time that we received the metaphysical basis for the assumption that historical study can produce true understanding. If you remove Hegel's metaphysics, much of the rationale for historical study ceases too. Thus, we reach the center of a problem which is crucial to modern metaphysics: What has history to do with philosophical understanding? Or, stated differently, how is the completion of the task of philosophy in any way connected with the solution of the seemingly insoluble puzzles latent in the vast accumulation of historical material?

Hegel accepts contradiction and motion as not only logical but as being the very heart of logic. Thus, whenever logic conceives of itself as timeless, it departs from Hegel and moves toward Plato. Motion and contradiction are matters apart from which process cannot be understood. Hegel is interested not in the simple facts of history, but only in the larger process. Beyond that, he is concerned with the way in which philosophical understanding takes up both simple facts and complicated processes and renders them rational by making them a part of the expression of the Spirit itself.

Reason is not to be understood apart from history, but only as expressed therein, so that both motion and the facts of history are transformed in this light. Reason is now seen to have a concrete embodiment; it is no longer an abstract logical dialectic. Plato wanted philosophers to return from philosophical study in order to apply their understanding to actual states and to men in process. Hegel's philosopher cannot understand himself or complete his philosophical task without becoming involved in the explanation of history as a whole. Any thinker who today seeks to find understanding in an historical process or inquiry is still essentially a follower of the Hegelian metaphysics.

To assume that the goal of reason is to be found in an historical understanding is a fundamental assumption of our time that is in need of basic reexamination. Perhaps this has already been begun in philosophy by existentialism and by forms of British empiricism. Such attempts also raise a further question, one which is crucial to Hegel himself. That is, does the process itself lead to its own completion? Since the process can be understood only as a whole, for Hegel to believe otherwise would be to cast a shadow on all philosophy, since everything that cannot be seen from an ultimate standpoint remains tinged with unreality.

Unlike either Plato or Aristotle, Hegel's is an all-or-nothing game. There are no "islands" of philosophical attention, no essences as distinct from accidents, no forms as intelligible apart from matter. Unless the whole is rendered complete and rational, all philosophy falls. Hegel's claim is by far the most ambitious and all-inclusive program ever set out for philosophy, but it is also, accordingly, the most subject to total doubt if any doubt about the possibility of its completion should creep in.

Hegel's belief in reason as fundamental to process accounts for the facts that he began as a theologian and that he does not offer theology a separate existence; he makes theology not only a part of philosophy itself but also its culminating point. God must be reached but, like Spinoza, Hegel believed that God must be understood "under the aspect of eternity." However, in Hegel's philosophy, eternity is no longer timeless, but is itself full of motion, complexity, and even violence. Unless this fact of dialectical activity is understood, philosophy can speak only partial truths, and the understanding of it will remain seriously incomplete. Clearly the culmination cannot transcend the process in the way that Plotinus's One transcended reason. If process is transcended, it is frustrated, for its aim is to reveal the whole as rationally connected. Thus, in order for process to be successful, the first principle of process must also be a culminating point. Reason's principle must not be outside the process, but must embody it in its fullness. Reason and motion exist on only a secondary level for Plotinus and perhaps even for Aristotle, but for Hegel they are ultimate features, embracing all things by completing and connecting them, not by transcending them.

Plotinus sought unity as his guiding metaphysical principle, and in order to do this he was forced to transcend reason. Earlier, through his emphasis on the Forms, Plato proposed a compromise with unity as a first principle, but this procedure left only some, and not all, of the world capable of being rationally explained. Now Hegel gives "unity" a new interpretation. Unity is not something in itself, but— just as Plato understood "Nonbeing" in terms of "Being" and "otherness"—Hegel argues that unity can really be understood only by reference to motion, dialectical development, and historical process. To say this is indeed to understand the One in terms of the Many. Perhaps, just as Plotinus is to be thought of as developing the extreme of Unity out of the compromise Plato proposed in his concept of the One and the Many, Hegel might be understood as accepting the ultimacy of the Many, but as interpreting Unity and Oneness through a new grasp of both reason and the self as developing process.

Still Hegel's goal is constantly haunted and is never free. A shadow is cast over it, not so much by the complex and comprehensive role which Hegel demands for philosophy—since skeptics are answered only by demonstrating the possibility of a task—as by the fear that the culmination of the process is to be found neither within philosophy itself nor within the structure of the process. If the "explanation" of process is to be found neither in the culmination of the process nor within its developing structure, no matter how profoundly it is grasped, then philosophy is held back from achieving its goal.

Does philosophy lack the missing link which is needed in order to render all things rational and intelligible in its own light? Should the explanation lie either "beyond" or "behind" the process itself, then philosophy would have to be quite radically reconceived, and its goal of becoming the animating spirit of all science would have to be modified. The unity and total comprehensiveness of philosophy's objective, as Hegel's vision revealed it, does not seem to be achievable. Nevertheless, the basic reexamination of the first principles upon which this—or any suggested view—rests has not yet been accomplished.

C. Motion and the Absolute

For centuries it had been traditional to exclude motion from the concept of an infinite God. Plato's "souls" were the source of motion, but they did not exist alone as first principles; and, if Plotinus's One contained motion, it was in a manner beyond rational laws. With Hegel, however, this situation is almost totally reversed. The *Absolute*, which is Hegel's first principle, is reached only as the result of a finite process fully extended, and the motion of the process itself is included as part of the Absolute without which it could neither exist nor be reached.

Our problem now becomes that of determining whether or not the Absolute is reached simply as a culmination of process. It is clear that Hegel's answer is an affirmative one. The process which leads to the Absolute patterns itself after organic development, so that the parts cannot be separated by reference to Hume's separate and distinct impressions (a solution which Whitehead adopts too). The aspects of process must be understood as parts of an interconnecting, interacting system. Aristotle wanted to inquire "beyond physics," but it is clear that a biological system, if understood in an evolutionary manner, is Hegel's starting point and model.

Motion itself thus becomes rational, despite Aristotle's views to the contrary, and this Hegelian proposal is perhaps his chief contribution to modern metaphysics. Motion is not rational if it is taken piecemeal, or if it is conceived of traditionally. Motion must be conceived of theoretically and taken in as a whole process; then and only then can it be seen as the heart of reason. The problem of freedom, as a result, receives an interesting solution in Hegel's theory, and again this answer is indicative of the basic principles in operation for Hegel, just as Kant's answer revealed Kant's principles.

According to Hegel, there is no meaning to freedom apart from a position in the organic process. Since the laws of the process' development are necessary, it follows that to be free means to grasp your position in the developing pattern and to lend yourself willingly to the full coming to birth of the Spirit at that time. In order to be free, you need a sense of history and of the laws which govern its development so that the exact needs and the "logic" of the moment can be grasped. Freedom does not mean to be self-determined in isolation; rather it means to desire rationally and to allow the self to be used by the spirit of its times. This is true even if the use of the self only provides the opposition without which there can be no power to the process of development.

The historical process becomes, in a real sense, divine. God does not sit apart and judge the process, as he did in the case of Noah, and find the whole thing at times not worth continuing. There are many negative and demoniac forces and factors present, to be sure; the dialectic of progress cannot move without such opposition. But the process of history—not the facts of any one event, but the movement of the whole—is given divine status as a direct expression of the Absolute. In fact, the Absolute is fulfilled in this unfolding of history, and the Absolute could not find full expression otherwise. This identification of the Absolute with the world process makes the rejection of God easier for those who cannot discern that the ultimate animating spirit of the world process is divine, and that in fact it is simply the necessary fulfillment of God's nature.

However, aside from this doctrine which has bound theology to an historical interpretation for over a century, perhaps the main problem resulting from Hegel's metaphysics is the question as to whether one can or cannot stand "outside the system" itself. On Hegel's own ground, the answer would seem to be "no." There are such things as parts and individual movements. There are such things as incomplete logical developments, and there are even those who aid philosophy by opposing it, and by offering the resistance without which further development could not occur. In the last analysis, however, it is not possible to stand outside this view of the world and to consider it as opposed to other views; according to the principles of this metaphysics, such a separation cannot be accomplished.

Since Hegel's time, many (including Marx) have denied our ability to "escape," or to stand outside the principles which govern our time. If it is true that such escape is impossible, then the only way to achieve understanding is to carry out the whole development; enlightenment cannot be found by proposing any alternative basis for our understanding. The major problem of Hegel's metaphysics is its claim to all-inclusive comprehensiveness. It is one view which cannot allow itself to be accepted simply as one approach among many first principles (Marxism cannot either). It cannot share philosophy with other radically different basic approaches except by considering each as a partial expression of itself. It must include all of philosophy's development within itself. Hegel's all-embracing theory has given philosophers reason to think it necessary to banish metaphysics in order to be free to pursue philosophy in some other way, but this is a strange inversion of the usual concept of metaphysics as the critique of every rigid view of philosophy.

D. The Unity of Metaphysics

The consideration of Hegel's metaphysics leads to perhaps the most pressing metaphysical problem of our age: the question as to whether metaphysics as a discipline is one thing only or nothing at all. This is the dilemma which Hegel has bequeathed to us. For those opposed to metaphysics, it is simpler if we answer that metaphysics is one thing, because then a certain critical argument—such as the logical positivist's proposal of a special criterion for "meaningfulness"—could hope to stop the whole process. For the Hegelian followers, the virtue of declaring metaphysics to be a single enterprise is that they can then hope to complete philosophy as a necessary science, and this outcome is still the objective of modern philosophy. If metaphysics is not a unified enterprise (a metaphysical norm that the positivists borrowed from science), then the lesson of Plato's *Parmenides* stands out clearly. Raising metaphysical questions will have a necessary tendency to engender an indefinite multiplicity of views in rapid succession. Now only an act of rational will—one that is able to stop the process at some definite point—can restrain philosophical thought from its natural tendency to produce an infinity of solutions.

The existence of alternatives to metaphysics as a unified activity is an unsatisfactory situation for the Hegelians. Interestingly enough, this is also true of the antimetaphysicians, since they still accept the most fundamental principle of Hegelian metaphysics as theirs: namely, the unity of all philosophical theory as the only alternative to intellectual chaos. As we said at the beginning of this inquiry, nothing can be more fundamental to philosophy than the interpretation and the position which are given to the concept of "unity." Plotinus and Hegel and the positivists have all given it primacy, although Hegel perhaps gave it its widest berth. If unity cannot be achieved by rising above reason, as Plotinus thought, but only by completing the full development of an organic whole, then Hegel supposed that the key to this development consisted in a new and dynamic concept of logic.

If the use of Kant's basic distinctions still stands as the major problem of metaphysics due to the restrictions imposed if the Kantian framework is accepted, then it is probably Hegel who creates metaphysics' major problem as far as doctrine is concerned for both those who reject and those who accept his scheme. Those who are critical of metaphysics are often still critical of its goal as Hegel so powerfully outlined it (see the discussion of Kierkegaard in the concluding chapter). All those who attempt this comprehensive goal are often persuaded of the soundness of Hegel's basic resolutions, as Whitehead shows in his philosophical emphasis on the centrality of "process."

Underneath the argument as to the value of Hegel's doctrine, however, still lies the problem of the unity of metaphysics. For if an historical or an evolutionary pattern is forced upon metaphysics without a critical analysis of the assumptions of such a framework, then metaphysics must be interpreted in quite special ways. Furthermore, if metaphysics is either a unity or nothing at all, then the possibility of shifting to alternative frameworks is ruled out, and the exclusive imposition of contemporary forms of interpretation becomes not dogmatism, but actually a necessity of thought.

If, however, metaphysics can be more multiple in its roots, our present situation is opened up to many different alternatives. The possibility for a variety of interpretive frameworks is made much wider, and this involves a greater allowance for the freedom of each individual thinker. Thus, even in considering metaphysics itself as an enterprise, the problem of the One and the Many enters in immediately and determines our approach to metaphysics. If unity is to be the chief goal of metaphysics, our interpretive approach is set for us. But if multiplicity is to inform the enterprise of metaphysics itself, the nature of the discipline is not fixed rigidly for us.

Our job is not to react against metaphysics either positively or negatively, for the first task of metaphysics is to determine the variety of the possible conceptions of the enterprise itself. When we have determined our alternatives, we must learn to hold onto one; we must use the power of reason and the decisiveness of will to follow out one conception of metaphysics as opposed to all of the other possibilities.

KIERKEGAARD
AND EXISTENCE

In spite of the natural logic which favors a chronological account, it may seem strange to devote the concluding chapter to a man who attacked metaphysics so violently. Kierkegaard not only professed to have nothing to do with metaphysics, but he called for its end in the interests of philosophy's health. We have already said that, in a real sense, it is impossible to argue against all metaphysics at once. This is particularly true because any view which argues against all metaphysics is itself only one outlook on philosophy, and thus rests on its own particular terminology and assumptions.

Yet, even if we wish to examine the antimetaphysicians, why choose Kierkegaard, since there are many other modern critics (the positivists, the skeptics, the empiricists, and the analysts) to pick from? We have asserted that one may begin negatively and still produce from this a positive route, a fresh direction, and, thus, a new metaphysics. If this is the case, why is it that a study of Kierkegaard might be more enlightening concerning a new direction for metaphysics than would any other approach?

A. The Individual and Isolation

In the first place, Kierkegaard is one of the few philosophers who has had an equal impact on both philosophy and theology. These are fields which have not been systematically connected during the modern period, and we have already suggested that a fruitful metaphysics might link religion to philosophy more closely in its theological usefulness. More than this, however, in actual fact, at least two major metaphysicians of recent times—Sartre and Heidegger—have taken a new orientation from the existentialism which stems from Kierkegaard, so there is some evidence that the foundation for a new metaphysics is actually present here. However, this may be true also of the other contemporary critical movements. For example, British philosophy, which has been analytic, seems inclined to return to at least some form of metaphysics. In any case, Kierkegaard presently offers the greatest impetus for sparking this revival. Therefore, in good metaphysical fashion, we should examine the starting point of the revival in Kierkegaard's work rather than any of the later expressions, such as those of Sartre and Heidegger, in which the new emphasis is mixed with many other strains—continental rationalism, phenomenology, philological analysis, and even a literary movement.

Kierkegaard puts great stress upon his category of the *individual*. That emphasis in itself is not news, for we have already noted a stress in modern philosophy upon the use of the self as a starting point. Still, when we contrast his conception of the individual with Hegel's, it is clear that Kierkegaard's new category is a quite radical departure. Kierkegaard stresses the self as existing in almost absolute isolation, whereas Hegel does not think the self can either exist or be defined except in a social and world-historical context. Quickly the differences in these approaches to the self become apparent, and the basic importance of this fact is that it indicates a dramatic contrast. Beginning with the self cannot guarantee us either agreement or similarity in technical doctrines, since the approach to the self is subject to disagreement.

In the modern search for certainty and finality, it once seemed that the self might provide a starting point immune from doubt, and thus be capable of securing for philosophy a fixed focal point. However, if the self now proves to be subject to a wide variety of interpretations as different from each other as those of Hegel and Kierkegaard, then a concentration on the self can offer no greater guarantee toward providing a basis of agreement in philosophical doctrine and procedure than any other starting point. In fact, what this consideration should lead us to suspect is that the self is not a neutral first principle possessed of some kind of special self-evidence.

Rather, the self is only defined by reference to various other principles that are adopted first, and these principles actually provide the basis for an understanding of it.

In Kierkegaard's case, it is clear that one of these principles is *isolation*. If the self is, at its core, cut off from all men and from all objective standards which can determine it, then this interpretation calls for a very different kind of understanding from the one Hegel offered in order to solve the self's problems. The self will now be very different from what it would be if it were able to define itself by its social and historical context. Philosophical doctrine, too, must take on a different role, for reason cannot necessarily penetrate to all things. The elaboration of doctrines, even if Hegel's grand enterprise were completed, might not touch the core of the individual. Instead, for Kierkegaard, the individual, despite all rational effort, is left alone to cope with his isolation.

B. Contingency and Decision

The inadequacy of purely rational effort does not render all philosophical construction valueless, although some types of construction must be abandoned because they do not reveal the situation that brings about the individual's final isolation. This view means that philosophy should be reconstructed to be of a special type in order to be applicable. At this point we reach the concepts which may have guided Kierkegaard's own interpretation of the self: *contingency* and *decision*. Hegel and most of the moderns before him sought necessity as the prime requirement in theory. Necessity may or may not characterize theory, Kierkegaard now replies, but it will either distort or miss the facts of existence if it is applied indiscriminately to the difficulties which face the individual. Kierkegaard does not yet generalize this warning into a principle for all Being, but he does say that contingency, instability, and uncertainty are the prime characteristics of existence as it is made known to man.

In a sense, both Spinoza and Hegel had known this too. Spinoza saw this condition of instability as stemming from an inadequacy of ideas, and from a failure to achieve control over emotion. On the other hand, Hegel saw the difficulties in existence as arising from a view of the world which had not yet been transformed by reason into a more comprehensive understanding. What Kierkegaard wants to assert against Spinoza and Hegel is the ultimacy of the immediate human situation. Kierkegaard stresses that the human situation is not something that exists merely to be transformed by philosophical understanding which shows it to be something different from what, in fact, it is.

Human deficiencies are revealed, instead, to be ultimate (thus involving a first principle); and philosophical speculation must conform itself to this unhappy fact rather than seek to transform it. Much, if not all, depends upon the starting point that is taken as the interpretive key. In Kierkegaard's understanding, this starting point is the individual, whose situation is one of isolation in the face of the ultimacies of decision. True, we are surrounded by a social context, but Kierkegaard thinks that this context is likely to be distorting if the individual looks to it for help. It is not that any man is ever free from other people. Rather, as Kierkegaard sees his situation, core decisions are not socially determined; they arise in individual isolation and must be met there.

That core decisions are individually met is due to the indeterminable state of things as far as human interests are concerned, whatever laws of a different kind may govern physical nature. To place man entirely in the context of nature—even if it is nature as elaborated by Hegel, or Substance as outlined by Spinoza—would be to distort man's nature and to insure his failure. This is because contingency in human affairs demands individual decisiveness. The form of any decision is not specifiable in detail by applying an external circumstance to the individual. This is true no matter how helpful, up to a point, the surrounding information may be. Anything which inhibits or blocks individual self-reliance and decisiveness will work to prevent man from assuming his position as human. To become a "man" is not a simple matter, nor does such a development come upon a man as the result of any forces external or superior to him. Rather, the status as a man is something formed by each individual, a distinctive creation which develops as his decisions firmly shape the form which the contingency around him takes.

As far as freedom is concerned, we have noted that other philosophers have developed philosophical contexts, wider than that of individual decision, within which freedom comes to be defined. Kierkegaard's assertion, however, is that the individual self, in its own immediate understanding of the problems of existence facing it, provides the only context in which freedom can be given its proper meaning. Anyone who supposes that the individual is not central overlooks the decisive importance of the human *will*, and fails to see how the movements of the will in fact can shape an individual's future as well as his self. It is the insistence upon some force other than that of the individual will that arouses Kierkegaard's antimetaphysical fury. He feels that abstract doctrines too often tend to explain away the contingent action of the will by regarding it as the by-product of some necessary force, and that this is done because such an interpretation fits more easily into some desired systematic goal. It is this kind of goal and the ambitions of human reason which Kierkegaard calls into account, just as Hume did, although Kierkegaard's reasons differ from Hume's.

C. The Subjective and Reason

To suit its own ulterior purposes, reason might like to set down rigid laws to govern the action of the human will, but this tendency is precisely what must be guarded against. There are preconceptions which Kierkegaard criticizes as causing this misleading attempt to take from the individual the contingent and decisive power of the will. One such preconception is the idea that an *objective* understanding can illuminate an area—namely the *subjective*—to which it not only does not apply but which it may actually falsify. Kierkegaard does not at all want to turn every issue into a subjective problem. To do so would be to distort the unique problems of subjectivity. All men live in two worlds and—in the objective world of facts—reasons, laws, and evidence determine the norms. But after this objective work is done, each individual must still work out his own relationship to such objective understanding as has been achieved; thus arises his "subjective problem."

All decisiveness for the individual lies in his will and in its subjective determination. To turn every issue into an objective question involving matters of fact or universal laws is to destroy precisely the needed decisive element—that is, the response and determination of the individual in his free choice. Kierkegaard does not deny that the objective situation and its facts guide the individual, but the important point is that the rationalists err in their goal of reducing all being to a necessary system. In particular, Kierkegaard contends, the Hegelian reliance on historical understanding, together with the assurance and guidance which such a pursuit is supposed to bring to the individual, is entirely misplaced. Not only is it not possible to complete the task of encompassing all history by a rational system, but to do so would distort man's situation in regard to the future. If the person is still alive, and not dead to existence, then the objective facts do not determine his response except in the most trivial cases. The more important the issue, the less do facts alone determine the ethical response. Love, for example, cannot be commanded.

Perhaps the most difficult task in understanding Kierkegaard is to determine the place and the function of reason. It is clear that for his modern predecessors—Descartes, Spinoza, and Hegel—reason is the center of philosophical development, and is perhaps all-important to life. Philosophy itself is the search for reasons, if it is not the very life of reason itself, and Kierkegaard's antirational tendencies have seemed to some to remove him from the sphere of philosophy, perhaps along with Nietzsche. To exclude him, however, begs the ultimate question of philosophy—the definition of the meaning and function of reason itself. And here it is clear that, although he works perhaps negatively and violently at times, Kierkegaard moves toward such a new definition of "reason." Clearly, reason still has the function of understanding, but for ethical and religious questions reason is not a sufficient determination in itself, although Kierkegaard's predecessors thought it could be.

If reason is not sufficient to produce decisiveness of will in crucial situations, then what does operate in order to make decision possible? Here we need to recognize the flexibility and contingency which Kierkegaard finds surrounding the self. He is not enough of a constructive metaphysician to make contingency itself characteristic of either God or Being. In fact, because Kierkegaard's metaphysical rebellion against Hegel keeps him from any such basic revision in first principles, most of the interior tension in his thought comes from the juxtaposition of his new grasp of the principles of human existence against a classical concept of God and Being. If such a metaphysical reconstruction could be provided, reason's position in the scheme of things might be more easily understood. As it is, human reason remains an alien in a foreign world, a world whose necessary and determinative reason would swallow up human decisiveness and individuality if it could. Against such an absolutizing "Reason," each individual "reason" must protest in order to protect its freedom.

D. Psychology and History

If Hegel made history both the queen of the sciences and the subject of philosophical understanding, Kierkegaard can be viewed as attempting to restore psychology as the key to all human interpretation. Kierkegaard often describes himself as a psychologist, and it is true that many of his most profound insights are based on a subtle exploration of interior states. His approach is reminiscent of that of Plotinus, except that Kierkegaard, in analyzing interior states, stresses the negative—despair, anxiety, dread. A different understanding is bound to arise from such an exploration. Just as it is characteristic of Plotinus to explain negative characteristics (examples of evil) in terms of positive qualities—that is, as consisting in a diminution or lack of good—so it is representative of the contemporary revolution to propose an understanding which is based on negative states induced by crisis. This theme aims at casting new light on positive structure drawn from the psychological exploration of states which threaten existence.

What is revealed by such a situation is the threat of the loss of meaning, and it quickly becomes evident that no objective or external circumstance or condition is able, of itself, to supply meaning. In this case, universal generalizations become more possible because they depend neither on the similarity of historical circumstances, nor even on the more elaborate Hegelian dialectic which would unite all apparently opposing situations into one scheme. Here the identity of all human existence is discovered: Identity is to be found only in those psychological states to which all men are subject, regardless and irrespective of social and temporal location.

The apparent absolute isolation of the individual is ultimate in that each man must face his situation with solitary decisiveness. But the individual is not absolutely alone, for psychological exploration reveals a common structure of existence which is participated in by all. The irony is that this common circumstance is located in the negative modes. Men are united more by negative forces than they are by positive states, since on the basis of the latter each man tends to go a different route. Crisis unites men in existence; calm days loosen the unity of existence and propel men toward incomprehensible multiplicity.

If we clearly locate the key to the unity of Being in the negative side of experience, we will be led to a view of history's place and importance rather different from Hegel's view. However, here Kierkegaard at last begins to provide a positive metaphysics for himself. He starts by asking what it is that is distorting, as far as the self's existence is concerned, if an apparoach is made through historical understanding. His answer is that in retrospect everything appears to be the result of necessity and of a determinative reason. From the historical point of view, the contingent element has been dropped out and whatever requires decision appears actually to have been determined in the past. Thus, the element of indeterminacy is lost (unless the historian can manage to view the past in the perspective of the future), and all decisiveness of human will is obscured. The past and the future do not really stand on equal ground. Since negative modes can reveal positive structure, we should reverse the process of our understanding. We must use our grasp of the future as the only basis upon which the past can be understood without distortion.

Where the self is concerned, now that the individual in his isolation is our focal point, the will is oriented toward infusing decisiveness into a contingent future which is as yet undetermined. This is a more accurate metaphysical model. Here history as a completed entity cannot help us, and our own insight into the nature of our existence in the present moment is much more instructive than any supposed rational pattern discoverable in history. We can understand a past event only on the basis of some penetration of the meaning of our own—and of every other man's—present existence. Lacking that, history will not be open to us, and it cannot serve as anything but a false guide.

Hegel perhaps found his key to the logic of dialectical development in his own contemporary grasp of existence, but Kierkegaard's understanding is such that it stresses contingency and individuality as opposed to necessity and universality. Because of this emphasis, Kierkegaard turns to the future for his model, and he denies the principles which, when assumed, had led Hegel to such fantastic explorations of, and hope in, complete historical understanding. Instead of history providing the key to the future, now the future is to provide the key to the past. The present moment gives us our clue for an approach to the future, and that is the way in which the past is now to be understood correctly.

E. The First Principles of Existence

The last thing in the world which Kierkegaard wanted to produce was a system, at least insofar as a system is understood to involve the necessity and the completion of reason's dominance. In fact, in spite of some inconsistencies in an attempt to tie his whole work together, Kierkegaard deliberately tries to produce a view that is not complete and ready for adoption. He does this so that the individual reader will be encouraged to decide questions for himself rather than to seek explanations ready-made in books. This stress on the necessity for repeated individual decision alters the conception of philosophy's task quite radically. Philosophy cannot guide a man unalterably to a single conclusion which exists alone as being rational—except at the cost of destroying his existence as an individual. Philosophy's function is more to prompt and to incite than it is to draw conclusions.

If this way of thinking is not a "system" in the Hegelian sense, can it still form the point from which interpretation proceeds? Kierkegaard's philosophical position is no less a metaphysics because of its lack of conformity to some one definition of the goals of that enterprise. Reason receives a new definition of its objectives and capacities, and it is no less reason for learning what it cannot do. Other principles—those of decision, will, and contingency—are on a par with reason in importance. It is quickly evident that we have returned to a situation of greater stress on multiplicity as a basic principle and have moved toward a relaxation of the demand for unity. In such a case of multiplicity, reason is less coercive and determinative. Yet, for all the difficulty that may be involved, it is existentialism's stress on *existence* which is distinctive. Existentialism refuses to have the truths which reason can find supersede individual existence and decision as a basis for interpretation. If the demands of reason are Hegel's basic guide, then Kierkegaard's first principle is certainly to be found in his understanding of existence. There his metaphysics lies.

There is a difficulty here, and yet it is also the decisive feature in Kierkegaard's approach. He seeks an understanding of existence through an exploration of psychological states, particularly those which have negative aspects productive of anxiety. Nevertheless, it certainly is not true that Kierkegaard is the first to offer an interpretation of existence. To assume so would be to beg the question, since all metaphysics leads to a characterization of existence. The question is: How is existence best approached, and what techniques and concepts express it with the least distortion? The burden of Kierkegaard's interpretation lies in the revelatory quality of the means which he proposed. His genius led him to ask whether an exploration of "dread" might reveal existence better than a search for the positive attributes ever could. Hegel made certain discoveries in the self about the dialectical operation of reason, and those discoveries gave him his key. Kierkegaard finds oppositions which have no rational mode of reconciliation, and this leads him to locate the key to existence in individuality and in its decisive power.

In a brief account it is not possible to attempt to reach any decision concerning these alternative metaphysical views, but reflection on the alternatives does raise—at the end—the chief problem of metaphysics: namely, that of locating its most fruitful beginning point. If this point actually were determined for us, then the history of philosophy (and probably of all human existence) would be quite different from what it is. It seems clear that the starting point, the terms employed, and the goal assigned to philosophy are not clear at the beginning. They must be worked out carefully, and the decisions reached here are all-important. Still, there are some who take philosophical procedure for granted—just as they take their lives for granted—simply as it comes to them. Yet, although not all men are metaphysicians seeking to question the first principles of all things, there still remain adventurous thinkers who persist in taking up this ancient task anew. Great as the odds against success may be, the possibility of providing a new beginning point for thought inspires some men so much that the metaphysical venture is again and again undertaken. From the opposition of creative intellects man can acquire new vision and greater power as man—if this opposition leads not to destructive conflict, but to the development of new ideas.

AUTHOR'S POSTSCRIPT

In this short work, which is intended simply to outline the problems of metaphysics, only one essential feature is lacking. Unfortunately, it is a crucial omission. In order to remedy this lack, I would have to give a constructive treatment of each one of these problems—that is, a treatment which moves toward "solutions," just as each classical theory did. Neither a statement of the problems nor an account of various approaches to them is a substitute for the detailed and careful construction that is necessary in order to deal with an issue in its perspective.

Of course, not every treatment must itself be either very complex or highly technical. That such an approach is essential is one possible assumption about philosophy, but it is one which we must not, as metaphysicians, grant without considering its alternatives. It is pertinent to remember that behind even a simple statement in metaphysics there must lie considerable detail of thought. It is this fact which accounts for the almost endless elaboration that is possible on the great metaphysical schemes.

Thus, within metaphysics, no final understanding of metaphysics is possible until the individual who seeks the understanding becomes involved himself in a constructive attempt to deal with some basic issue. Perhaps much of the criticism of metaphysics, particularly if it misses the mark, comes either from a failure to experiment or from a failure to establish a concrete setting for an abstract problem among the complexities of the critic's own thought. These failures do not occur in the great metaphysical critiques—for example, those by Hume or Kant. Each metaphysician must clearly work out his own criticisms until they become a firm set of basic principles. In that sense, each critic reaches his own metaphysics.

Although I have attempted an interpretation of various metaphysical concepts many times in print—otherwise I would not presume to discuss the problems of metaphysics—still, this is no place to state the details of my own metaphysical conclusions. A work intended as an introduction to the problems of metaphysics has a different objective, and yet it is obvious that even to state the problems, much less to give an account of them, is already to reveal certain things about the author's own metaphysical views.

At this point one essential "problem" of metaphysics presents itself. Each reader should state in detail just what it is about any given author's approach and statement that reveals that author's own first principles and which, in accordance with good metaphysical procedure, the reader thinks must not go unchallenged. To do this with an author is perhaps the most important philosophical task that the reader should assume. This task may very well be something which a philosopher cannot do for himself, for his own first principles may be so basic to him that they can be treated in detachment only by another. Fortunately, philosophy is a corporate enterprise; therefore, we can correct each other. We can see ourselves in contrast, if only we have the courage to look outside our own circle of like-minded philosophical friends.

As Aristotle said long ago of the task of metaphysics, individually we seem to fail, but together we may succeed. Sometimes, in noting individual failures and in discovering particular obscure spots in some one metaphysical theory, we are blinded, and consequently we fail to see the greater success of the enterprise when it is taken as a whole. However any other branch of philosophy may proceed, this possibility should lead metaphysicians to conclude that metaphysics can be done only on a broad comparative basis. If it limits itself to one approach, metaphysics fails to achieve its central task—namely, a comparative criticism of all first principles and basic assumptions.

Yet it would seem to be a necessity of metaphysical inquiry that the inquirer should attempt this task constructively for himself. He must do this at the possible risk of misunderstanding the whole enterprise. If the questions of metaphysics are ever to take on clear meaning, a statement of these problems must be undertaken by the one who wants to understand. Since no single definitive statement of any philosophical problem exists in a form accepted by all, this necessity to reformulate the problem at the very beginning is not a minor matter. Rather, it is perhaps all-important to the conclusion reached.

Since we first observed Plato at work discussing various approaches to questions in his *Dialogues*, we have seen that the most difficult problem for the philosopher is to find the right way to formulate the question. The only intolerable philosophical dogmatism is an assumption that one formulation of a problem is itself final or somehow beyond challenge. If we do not question the formulation of the issue ourselves, soon someone will arise to do it for us—unless, of course, we have limited ourselves to trivialities which are not even worth the effort to challenge.

One reason for the widespread lack of understanding with regard to the problems of metaphysics today may be an inherited inhibition against attempting their solution. To mention this possibility is not to prejudice any constructive attempt to reach a conclusion—even if the result of such an attempt is the lack of a conclusion—but it is to argue that the only successful route by which metaphysical problems can take on meaning is through a willingness on the part of the inquirer to become a metaphysician, at least for a time. This is so because we begin metaphysics with no defined and agreed upon set of general problems. Instead, the problems of metaphysics take on particular form only as they are actually explored. Historical writings provide the raw material for our work, but they do not in themselves lead to a clear and singular formulation of the issues. To provide that grasp is the individual's responsibility, as has always been the case in metaphysics.

If it is not a fault, at least it is a notorious fact that philosophers tend to ask more questions than they answer. An understanding of why this fact is true may be the best possible insight into the nature and the task of philosophy. Thus, without any attempt to answer them, it may be best to leave our reader with a few questions at the end. He can then make his own beginning point if he chooses.

Where shall we turn in the present day to look for a new beginning to metaphysics? If we have accurately presented what in fact metaphysics has been in the past, what does this tell us about what it might be today or tomorrow? Concededly, it is an exaggeraton to say that philosophers only ask questions and never answer them. For in discussing metaphysics we have already said that the formulation of the question is not itself neutral; rather, it already contains most of whatever answer the philosopher may eventually come to provide.

As indications of future direction, what do the formulations of the two questions above—with which we propose to leave the reader—suggest to us about their answers? In the first place, metaphysics is not simply a past enterprise, but is an ever present one. Thus, its renewal is possible in any time, including ours. Furthermore, the account which we have given indicates that metaphysics is never a wholly contemporary affair, but that, whenever one embarks upon it, he immediately becomes (or should become) contemporary with every past metaphysician who has gone in search of new first principles which will allow a new development of theory.

However, it should also be clear by now that we reject historical determinism or any limitation which binds us to some one set of principles which supposedly are inherent in our time. That assumption is so vast—and yet recently it has been so prevalent—that the first way to assert the metaphysician's freedom to examine all first principles might be to declare his independence from a theory of contextual determinism. At least the metaphysician should declare this independence until he has had a chance to examine that theory and its assumptions. Then he can vote for or against its continuation on the basis of his examination.

DISCUSSION
QUESTIONS

Chapter I

1. Why do you think that philosophy as an enterprise is always in question?

2. Although many philosophers have objected to doing metaphysics at all, why do you think it is still so very much alive and vital?

3. Do you think Plato is right in not accepting immediate experience as explanatory on its own terms?

4. Do you think that, if we are to have first principles for thought, they must be certain?

5. Can you think of a way in which we can settle the skepticism over metaphysics once and for all? If so, how?

Chapter II

1. How do we decide what the problems of metaphysics actually are and how they are to be phrased?

2. Why are *Being* and *Nonbeing* special problems unlike any other questions we deal with?

3. Why is it important to determine whether or not we are completely bound by time?

4. Explain the search for *substance* and how it is related to the question of whether or not there really are any *accidents*.

5. Do you think *God* and *freedom* pose questions which can be simply decided by a direct approach? If so, how?

Chapter III

1. How is it that we come to know *Being, Nonbeing,* and *Becoming*, and what causes us to distinguish between them?

2. In dealing with metaphysical problems, how does the principle of *the Good* enter in, and how does it function for Plato?

3. As Plato describes it, in what sense is the soul rational and in what sense is it not?

4. How does *the One and the Many* become a problem in metaphysics? Do you see how a solution to this problem is important for other questions?

5. When you consider Plato and *Being*, which principle would you actually put as "first" in Platonic thought?

Chapter IV

1. In what sense does *metaphysics* really mean *first philosophy?* What is *first philosophy?*

2. Do you think metaphysics is connected to the idea of understanding a thing through its causes? How can one decide how many types of causes there are?

3. How can we decide how many categories there are and what ones are necessary to characterize events?

4. How do we know whether we must set a limit on philosophy's scope, and what determines how such a limit is set?

5. Why does Aristotle introduce God? What kind of a God does he feel he needs, and why?

Chapter V

1. What problem does *transcendence* pose for philosophy, and why is the question bound to come up in metaphysics?

2. In developing a set of metaphysical principles, why is the demand for unity bound to arise, and what issues are at stake in meeting it?

3. What is it that brings about a challenge of reason's ability, and how can any "solution" really lie "beyond reason"?

4. In considering the function of first principles, what place does the problem of evil have, and how is it possible to solve this problem?

5. In what sense is it possible to provide a reason for creation or an explanation of why Being was formed in this way?

Chapter VI

1. What is the peculiar problem of "modern" metaphysics that sets it apart from the metaphysics of previous ages and defines our present starting point?

2. Why do you think some philosophies have sought *certainty*, and how crucial to metaphysics do you think this concept is?

3. Can we find any starting point which cannot be challenged? What are the consequences for philosophy if we cannot?

4. Is the self really the "natural" starting point? What advantages and disadvantages do you see in this assumption?

5. Is thought something in itself which can be treated as a self-contained object? What consequences follow if we begin with the structure of things rather than with thought?

Chapter VII

1. How can we discover what is "capable of independent existence," and why is doing so central to metaphysics?

2. Even if we manage to provide a criterion for certainty, why is that not the end of the matter rather than simply a signal for debate?

3. What are the advantages and disadvantages in opening philosophy up to consider the widest possible range of possible entities?

4. How does *freedom* come to be a problem, and in what way is it dependent on or independent of metaphysics?

5. How does *ethics* become involved in metaphysics? Is it better or worse to keep the two issues separate?

Chapter VIII

1. What is the issue over the use of technical vocabulary in metaphysics, and what alternatives do we have?

2. Of what importance is *experience* to metaphysics, and how can we go about determining what it can and cannot contain?

3. Does metaphysics necessarily demand a "two world" theory? In such a theory, how can we determine the way in which these worlds are related?

4. What gives rise to *skepticism* in philosophical theory? Can skepticism be overcome?

5. When we discover what a man's basic assumptions are, what is the best way to proceed to deal with them?

Chapter IX

1. If it is metaphysics' job to get at *reality*, how does it go about distinguishing what is *appearance?*

2. In what ways do *logic* and *spirit* become a part of metaphysical concern, and how can we determine their relationship to thought?

3. How are *reason, history,* and *dialectic* related, and what difference does it make to metaphysics how we choose to approach these concepts?

4. How can we decide what role *motion* has and whether it might be excluded in some parts of Being?

5. What happens to metaphysics as an enterprise, and to its goals, if we decide that it has a variety of acceptable forms?

Chapter X

1. What can we learn about metaphysics from those who have opposed it, the antimetaphysicians?

2. What difference to metaphysics does it make as to what context we choose in order to understand the *individual?*

3. What places do *contingency* and *decision* have in metaphysics, and why are they treated as either primary or secondary?

4. If all questions cannot be decided *objectively*, what does this do to the goals of metaphysics?

5. What determines the roles which *psychology* and *history* will play in developing a metaphysics?

ADDITIONAL
READINGS

Aristotle. *Metaphysics*. Trans., Richard Hope. 1960.

Descartes, René. *Discourse on Method and Meditation*. Trans., L. J. Lafleur. 1960.

Hegel, Georg Wilhelm Friedrich. *Reason in History*. Trans., Robert Hartman. 1953.

Heidegger, Martin. *An Introduction to Metaphysics*. Trans., Ralph Manheim. 1961.

James, William. *Pragmatism*. 1955.

Kant, Immanuel. *Prolegomena to Any Future Metaphysics*. 1950.

Kierkegaard, Sören. *Philosophical Fragments*. Trans., David Swenson and Howard Hong. 1962.

Leibniz, Gottfried Wilhelm von. *Monadology and Other Philosophical Essays*. Trans., Paul and Anne Schrecker. 1965.

Plato. *Parmenides*. Trans., F. M. Cornford. 1950.

Plato. *The Sophist*. Trans., F. M. Cornford. 1957.

Plotinus. *Works*. Ed., A. H. Armstrong. 1964.

Sartre, Jean Paul. *Being and Nothingness*. Trans., Hazel Barnes. 1966.

Sontag, Frederick. *Divine Perfection: Possible Ideas of God*. 1962.

Sontag, Frederick. *The Existentialist Prolegomena: To a Future Metaphysics*. 1969.

Taylor, Richard. *Metaphysics*. 1963.

Walsh, W. H. *Metaphysics*. 1963.

Whitehead, A. N. *Process and Reality*. 1929.

INDEX

Time, 21-22, 28, 50, 84, 94, 108
Transcendence, 55-65

Unity, 20-21, 32, 33, 41, 46, 55-60, 63,
    64, 66, 74, 109, 112, 113, 123

Unmoved Mover, 49, 50, 52, 53, 57,
    58, 64, 65, 83, 107

Whitehead, Alfred North, 110, 113
Will, 89, 118, 119, 122, 123